SELECTED ESSAYS & REFLECTIONS

This is Tantra

Sundari Ma

Copyright © 2025 All rights are reserved, and no part of this publication may be reproduced, distributed, or transmitted in any manner, whether through photocopying, recording, or any other electronic or mechanical methods, without the explicit prior written permission of the publisher. This restriction applies to any form or means of reproduction or distribution.

Exceptions to this rule include brief quotations that may be incorporated into critical reviews, as well as certain other noncommercial uses that are allowed by copyright law. Any such usage must adhere to the specified conditions and permissions outlined by the copyright holder.

This is Tantra

To my beloved friends who keep insisting on their anonymity.

You bring magic to each coffee chat and laughter to challenging days. You steady me when storms rise, cheer me on when I falter. You have filled my days with wild possibilities. You uplift my work with a love that asks for nothing in return.

This journey and this book, none of it would exist without you. Your kindness and strength changed the way I walk. I bow to your humility and service to your fellows.

Thank you. I love you.

TABLE OF CONTENTS

SUFI PRAYER. 7

Introduction 9

AUM 13

TEACHERS & SAINTS . . . 15

The Subtle Art of Devotion; or Just Lose Yourself in Love . . . 17

The Other Manhattan Project 25

The Tao of Anandamayi Ma 39

The Knowledge that Liberates and the Teacher Who Set Me Free. 45

IMMERSIONS & TRANSFORMATIONS . . . 51

From the Mountain Top to the Valley. 53

Stille Nacht, Heilige Nacht. 65

Therein Lies the Peace of God 71

Man vs the Goddess. 77

GODS & GODDESSES . . . 85

Rumi was a Savage; or She is Black 87

Lakshmi and the Utpatti of Soma 99

Jai Sita Ram and The Snake Who Ate Its Own Tail. . 107

Laying Down Arms: Chhinnamasta and the Battle of the Sexes 115

Acacia Trees and The Living Field of Bhuvaneshwari . .123

Glossary of Key Tantric Terms 136

Bibliography 139

This is Tantra

SUFI PRAYER

Let us begin in the name of God, the Compassionate, the Merciful, the Restorer of all things in their pristine glory, the Bestower of the All-Sufficient power of Healing.

Let us invoke the Divine Spirit, the quickener of Life.

Let us invoke the Archangel Raphael and all the angelic hosts occupied with the healing ministry.

Let us invoke the Messiah, the Beloved's response to the suffering cry of the planet.

Let us invoke all those who have come to the succor of humanity in times of distress; who have brought greater Life, greater Light, greater Love to replace humankind's suffering, darkness and despair.

Let us invoke Osiris, Imhotahep, Hermes, Ascelepius, Hippocrates, Orpheus, Pythagoras, Mahadeva Shiva, the Lord Buddha, the Quan Yin, the Lord Zarathustra, the Mother Mary, Jesus Christ, St. Francis, Avicena, Paracelsus, St. Germaine.

Let us invoke all others, known and unknown, who have held aloft the Light of Truth through the darkness of human ignorance.

This is Tantra

INTRODUCTION

What a year it has been! I never thought I'd end up living in the desert of Dubai, where the haunting beauty of the Islamic call to prayer opened a whole new chapter in my life.

The essays in this book were written over the past twelve months. Though not presented in chronological order, they do in some ways chronicle my transition from long-time student to teacher of Tantra.

Along the way, I have met many new people and learned many new sayings. *Where the rubber meets the road*, is one of them.

What began as a relatively innocent invitation to visit Dubai and hold space for a weekend meditation gathering soon became the ultimate test of all the teachings and practices I had learned and absorbed over the past few decades. Could the full promise of Tantra truly reach people amid the everyday trenches of modern life? Could it resonate with stressed-out parents and challenged children, with busy professionals from all walks of life—with men and women of deep faith, rooted in their religion of birth, and even with those who reject religion altogether?

The rubber did, indeed, meet the hot Dubai roads this year. Some of the essays in this book reflect on the powerful moments, raw experiences and personal insights from that wild journey.

Another phrase: *drinking from a firehose!*

The weekend turned into another... and then another, until I found myself living in an apartment near the yoga studio where the tantric gatherings were happening several times per week and nearly every weekend.

It is only now, during the relatively quiet summer break in my hometown at the foot of the Black Forest mountains in Germany, that I can lean back and fully take in the magnitude of all that has unfolded this year.

Grace. A storm of Grace in the middle of the desert. It feels important to bear witness to these kinds of moments, so that others may share in them, rejoice and wonder at the possibilities promised by the spiritual life. This book is my best attempt to capture some of those moments and to share them in the same spirit in which they were experienced: wonder, gratitude, and, at times, awe.

Although I've received a great deal of support this year from many people, I feel the need to single out one person. His name is Alex Thomas. He claims to be my student and editor.

Though he insists on calling me his teacher, I see him as a truly remarkable human being and a master in his own right. And I feel incredibly fortunate that we share such a deep passion for the tantric path: for the ancient teachings and traditions, for uplifting those around us, and for the English word.

He also happens to be, in my eyes, a brilliant and refreshingly original writer. His words carry a grounded humility, the insight of a mystic, a sharp and often hilarious wit that echoes the maturity of a man who has lived a full life, travelled the world and made peace with its dark crevices. He has the incredible gift of seeing light and love everywhere he looks. And whatever he may call me, I choose to call him my dear friend whom I can't thank enough for his support.

I want to take a moment to acknowledge him here, because without him, this book simply wouldn't exist. In many ways, he's a co-author and his voice appears directly in a few of the articles, though usually anonymously, just as he prefers.

This dynamic between Alex and me at times created an interesting if not fascinating creative tension. Within the writing process, but more importantly within the spiritual teachings themselves. This terrain, the interplay between the masculine and the feminine is what makes this book so profoundly precious to me. This interplay lies in the very heart of Tantric philosophy in the Shiva-Shakti relationship, and, of course, at the very core of life itself. In an age when men and women are so often strained to hear one another, working with Alex on these essays has brought me a new depth of insight and reverence for some of the great mysteries.

So thank you Alex, and to you, dear reader, thank you. Thank you for holding this book in your hands, and for reading these words. Through you, this work becomes an offering... back into the river of Life.

May some of these words fan your inner flame and spark your remembrance.

With you on the path,

Sundari Ma.

Freiburg, Germany, July 21, 2025

This is Tantra

Shri Yantra, the most revered of all tantric yantras, is a mystical diagram of the cosmos. This sacred geometric form offers a vision of the totality of existence, as the union of the masculine and feminine principle, enabling the tantric practitioner to internalize its symbols and realize their unity with the cosmos.

A U M

'In the beginning was the Word, and the Word was with God, and the Word was God.' He said.

What does that even mean? I wondered.

Sitting by the campfire that night, I listened to the old man revel in my questions for hours. He waxed eloquent about the way it one day was and the way it one day would be again. The Word! He exclaimed excitedly. The way of things! He almost shouted.

He talked all the whilst she sat silent beside him.

Her madraga was so black I barely made her figure through the smoke, but for her eyes. Wide open and innocent but unyielding; glowing the red and orange of the flames flickering between us.

I couldn't hear him anymore. Her gaze pulled me into a place so deep and so far and so thick with velvety silence. Everything was gone, the questions, the old man, the desert and the fire, everything; all what a man could want or care for was gone too. Nothing to hold to except the faintest echo of her stilted breathy voice, uttered like she had never before spoken.

This, she whispered, is Tantra.

-AT

This is Tantra

Selected Essays & Reflections

TEACHERS

&

SAINTS

This is Tantra

The Subtle Art of Devotion; or Just Lose Yourself in Love

A Journey to Siddhi Ma in Vrindavan

"Out of infinite compassion, come the full spectrum of relationships for tantric practice. Heavy emphasis on practice. Siddhi Ma and Neem Karoli were incredible beings, capable of living the highest form of devotional love with an intensity few of us can ever experience except by moment. They inspire, we perspire. And toil, inching forward and sometimes sliding backward but always guided by the lamplight of Grace; these luminous souls gently urging, this way... this is the way home."

Neem Karoli Baba, Maharaj-ji or just Baba is by now part of western folklore. Beautiful stories about this saintly figure can be found all over the internet and in books; this article then is my contribution to the canon of first-hand eyewitness accounts of miracles, big and small.

SPRING 2006

I was visiting with a dear friend on the Greek island of Corfu. She had just returned from a trip to California and was eager to share stories about the people she had met there. These people, she said, had once been with Neem Karoli Baba, a person who I had only vaguely heard of.

She gave me a photograph and I started to cry. Not because of the gift but something about the image of the man pierced my heart. The photo that had been glued on a rectangular piece of wood showed a portrait of Baba.

I couldn't stop looking at his face. His mischievous smile. The tenderness of a man wrapped in a blanket gently gazing into my eyes.

Come to India. A sudden and lightning-like sense of clarity rushed through my being and reflected the sweetest and warmest of feelings radiating from my heart. I have to go to India.

My life had just been upended by a photograph. Within a few months I was on my way to visit Neem Karoli's ashram in Vrindavan, a small town in northern India.

The waves of anxiety began when I took my seat after boarding. I had planned everything up and until I got onto that flight to Delhi. Obsessively even, totally focused on getting to Vrindavan and visiting the ashram. So intense was the drive that it never occurred to me what I would do once I arrived at the ashram. What to bring or how to dress, what to even say or if I would be even welcomed!

It was a sobering moment. Sitting in that tension between completely irrational, and yet a profound sense, deep within me and completely irresistible; this ineffable moment that has been a hallmark of the spiritual transformation in my life since.

I was traveling to India because of a photograph. There is simply no way of explaining this calmly to people that have loved you your whole life.

By then I knew a little more about Neem Karoli Baba. He had become a popular figure in the west with notable teachers in the spiritual scene like Ram Dass speaking and writing about him. I learned that he had passed away only a few months before I was born; that many still visited his ashram as a pilgrimage. What intrigued me most was that his longtime devotee, Siddhi Ma, still lived at the ashram and I might have a chance to see her.

I visited the ashram every day for the next two weeks. On entering the grounds, the ashram guardian raised his hand to greet me. Black shining hair accurately cut, beige shirt neatly tucked into his pressed pleat trousers, sitting in his office room some days or on a wooden chair in front of it on others.

Then walking past the women in simple cotton saris busy sweeping the soil in front of the Hanuman temple. One hand placed on their backs, gaze fixed on the hand-made broom, they moved rhythmically across the courtyard.

Each day, streams of people flowed through the gates, carving out moments from their busy lives to pause and fold their hands in prayer. A wide spectrum of human emotion unfolded before me: quiet desperation in a mother's eyes, joy in a grandmother's whispered prayers, fatigue etched into a laborer's face. Despite the diversity of these feelings, they seemed to weave together like threads in Baba's warm blankets; everyone and all of it, right there in an ashram not much bigger than a children's schoolyard.

Every morning on arriving, I would settle beside the small Baba *mandir*, (dwelling place of the inner self). I became a quiet witness to the ashram's day life, soaking up the atmosphere and hoping for some kind of a sign. I tuned into the rhythm of the arati that was performed with cymbals, bells and chanting each morning and evening, the ebbing and flowing of the visitors, the sound of brooms and barking dogs.

Despite the serenity around me, the anxiety persisted. Did I belong here? Was I just an observer? Where was my place in life? I had no idea why I was here or what exactly I was looking for. I had *come to India*, and sat on the ashram grounds every morning wondering what am I supposed to do now that I'm here. All these questions dissolved when I saw Siddhi Ma for the first time.

I couldn't see her at first. It was the anticipation building in the crowd that alerted me. The stirring and the chattering; hushed whispers of Ma and the crowd began to move towards the garden.

Siddhi Ma appeared in the early afternoon. Here, words can only deceive and will not capture the grace of that moment. What really to say about encountering a holy being; she wore a white *kurta* and headscarf? She smiled warmly?

Neem Karoli Baba was a very rare man, a true saint they said and this woman stood by his side for decades. *Traveling with him, tending to his daily needs, cooking Moong Dhal for him because he loved it so much...* She was devotion in a blazing white dress; her eyes glistened of milk and honey, her smile nourished the great Brahmaputra river and all of its tributaries and when she came out that day the elephants in faraway Assam trumpeted together in unison. A moment in her presence and the trajectory of my entire life had just been set. That dear reader, is the power of a saint.

I had received what I came here for. Perhaps not so much in the kind of rational way I would be able to explain to my family back home but deep within myself I had touched a place of *knowing*. I knew I would return to India many times and my *dharma would* unfold from here. New teachers would come into my life at the right times and guide me deeper into Vedic knowledge and later, yogic and tantric scripture. That gnawing feeling I had since my flight over had been replaced by a sense of profound peace and purpose.

And then joy. I was overwhelmed with gratitude for my friend and her gift that had led me to that moment. But even then, Baba was not quite done.

On my final evening in the ashram, I meditated next to Baba's wooden bed. Unexpectedly, a young woman came towards me, gently took my hand and guided me into the inner sanctum of the ashram. It was a tiny room and people were gathering. Most of them were sitting on rugs, some in plastic chairs that were lined up at the back of the room. Beneath the windows facing the garden, seated on one of the carpets was Siddhi Ma.

There was nothing that set her apart, no entourage, no protective circle of followers, no cushioned seat, no garlands of flowers, not even a drink by her side. She was simply present, chatting with people, patting their heads, smiling, offering hugs, and holding their hands. There she was, a mother to all freely breathing her fullness into a crowded room.

In one of Ram Dass's many Maharaj-ji stories, he speaks of the rare occasions where Baba would give him specific guidance. This particular one came only after Ram Dass pleaded with him for a teaching. After considering his pleas for a moment, Baba pulled on Ram Dass's beard and whispered into his ear: *Love everyone and tell the truth.*

Siddhi Ma did not need to speak that night because she was loving everyone and she was truth. And this was when the power of Neem Karoli astonished me once more.

I heard some shuffling in the room and saw an old man painfully and ever so slowly getting up from his plastic chair. His body looked frail. He was wearing marine-blue cotton pants and a brown shirt that had seen better days. The room fell silent as he ambled towards Ma. Nobody helped this man.

Time seemed to slow and everyone watched the scene unfold.

He was barefoot and each small step seemed to creak a different joint. His face though, looking into her eyes was absolute radiance and splendor.

A single tear began to roll down Siddhi Ma's cheek as he approached.

Standing a few feet from her, he began to bend. Then he began to kneel. Once on his knees, he began to lean forward and prostrate himself before her. His forehead pressed against the cold concrete floor and his bent arms were stretching to touch her feet.

Siddhi Ma placed both her hands tenderly on his head and a few people wept quietly.

I intuited something then, that in the infinite possibilities of an exuberant universe, Neem Karoli was with that man in that moment. That it was in fact Baba himself returning to his ashram that night. Deep inside the heart of the prostrated man, Baba was showing Siddhi Ma some devotion of his own.

Witnessing the power of absolute devotion reverberates in my heart to this day. It has propelled me forward in challenging times and fueled my spiritual practice. It has been the energy behind every intense transformational period and major decisions in my life.

The inspiration from my trip to the ashram led me towards the path of reverence and inner worship, Tantra. That of all the spiritual paths one can take, it is Tantra that is so intimately engaged with the relational. One heart to another.

It is devotion not to the ineffable and unmanifest or the field of infinite potentiality, but very much towards *this here now*. The agony and ecstasy of us. The delirious folly of the cosmos as a melting ice cream cone; try and figure it all out or savor it fully before it disappears.

Out of infinite compassion, come the full spectrum of relationships for tantric practice. Heavy emphasis on *practice*. Siddhi Ma and Neem Karoli were incredible beings, capable of living the highest form of devotional love with an intensity few of us can ever experience except by moment. They inspire, we perspire. And toil, inching forward and sometimes sliding backward but always guided by the lamplight of Grace; these luminous souls gently urging, *this way... this is the way home*.

For many, Neem Karoli Baba is not considered a teacher. A saint maybe but not a teacher in the way most people understand that role. There are some tantalizing nuggets however; like in this story Krishna Das shares, possibly being the rarest of public teachings from Maharaj-ji. A meditation lesson no less!

Paraphrasing, when asked how to meditate, Baba replied: *Meditate like Jesus.*

When asked how Jesus meditated, Baba first was silent, then began to weep and said simply: *He lost himself in love.*

'When there is Love, what else is needed?' He asked.

'More Love,' She replied.

-Sundari Ma

This is Tantra

The Other Manhattan Project

·

Sally Kempton and the Shakti Revolution

"A lone woman from New York, walking tall, headlong into a raging storm of indignity and suffering; noblesse unwavering because beneath the dignity and grace, the warmth and wisdom could only be the fiercest of wills. The kind of indomitable spirit and unfaltering faith needed to persevere through the most demanding of challenges. Pioneering qualities that have inspired and paved the way for this next generation to carry her work."

Few people outside of dedicated spiritual communities and journalism will know her name, but one or two generations from now, Sally Kempton may well be remembered as the woman who helped midwife the world into a new era.

Or, to put it more simply, Sally played a vital role in bringing Shakti from the jungles of Maharashtra to the streets of New York City and Carmel, USA. In doing so, Sally, along with the lineage behind her and the peers of her era who embodied this power, kindled a spiritual revolution that is today starting to break into the mainstream.

For those unfamiliar with the term Shakti and the concepts of the Divine Feminine, I explore both in this article. As a former student of Sally's, I also interviewed two fellow students about Sally, her remarkable gifts as a teacher and what her legacy means to those of us who have studied with her and carry on her work.

In the crowded bookstore of our local train station, my eyes fell on the cover of the new American *Yoga Journal* edition. In bright yellow, the words *'Divine Feminine'* were spread across the page, and I knew I had to buy this magazine. I felt an excitement surging through my body that surprised me.

The article, written by Sally Kempton, explored the Hindu goddesses, the archetypal feminine powers of consciousness, and how we can invoke and work with them. The signs couldn't have been clearer—something within me *needed* to learn more about the divine feminine, and I knew I had to connect with the author.

Two weeks later, I was on my first live-group-call with Sally, on a course on deity practice.

Welcome everyone. This is Sally. I'm delighted to share the space of this virtual container for the next few weeks with you. One of the real gifts that I've discovered in the process of teaching telecourses, is that one of the qualities of the goddess, one of the ways we experience the sacred feminine is as the connectivity between all of us. In other words, the sacred feminine is dancing through the particles of electrical impulses of information packets that are flowing between us and that as we get closer to one another, as we get to know the nature of this particular sacred community, we'll start to feel her presence very much as a space that flows between us.

On that call, Sally could have talked about her favorite recipe or read out the New York train schedule line by line—it wouldn't have mattered.

I didn't know about her lineage of great Siddha masters at that time, a detail I have since come to realize is very important.

Sally wasn't visible. It was an audio call, like all her sessions. Her voice was warm, melodious and vibrant. It reminded me of something golden and liquid, honey-like. I felt this inward pull which created a slight feeling of drowsiness.

Suddenly her voice was everywhere. It was the thread and the carpet at once, a flying one that transported me into new terrain of my consciousness. Sally started talking and I began floating.

This is the very power of the Siddha masters. For those unfamiliar with these beings, or the awakening of Shakti (aka Kundalini awakening), a bit of background is essential.

In this context, Shakti represents the revealing power of the divine feminine that initiates the Kundalini process, leading to the unravelling and transformation of human consciousness within the individual.

From a certain vantage point, all spiritual practice—whether in a church pew, at a mosque, yoga studio or around a shamanic campfire—

is concerned with this matter of awakening. The term implies that something within a person lies dormant and that, through a process, ritual or devotional act, what is asleep will awaken, which is regarded as a beneficial development.

Not always.

While most awakenings are gentle and evolutionary—easily and gradually integrated into a person's life—some can be radically transformative and pose potential challenges. A sudden and powerful collision with the Absolute, experienced without proper preparation, understanding, or guidance, and without the necessary physiological and psychological structures in place, can not only be risky for the individual but may also negatively affect those around them.

It is perhaps for this reason that the topic of Kundalini awakening has been hidden from the general public and mainstream spirituality for so long. Unlike today's popular self-help style 'spiritual awakening' where there is a collaboration between the person and a process within a certain structure, the awakening of Shakti is to self-improvement what a tornado would be to kitchen remodeling.

Fortunately, the process can be safe-guarded when a heart-to-heart connection between a dedicated student and a capable teacher is established—when there is love and trust. The awakening of Shakti is an act of grace, often ignited through the connection with a teacher who has undergone the process firsthand. Under ideal circumstances, the wisdom, experience, and consciousness of the teacher, combined with the preparedness of the student, provide a level of protection and support for what is about to unfold.

There are many names for these special teachers that can ignite this process, and for the sake of simplicity and to honor the tradition, I will refer to these beings as Siddha masters.

Siddha is a term widely used in Indian culture. It means "one who is accomplished" or "perfected one." It refers to those masters who have achieved liberation or enlightenment—who are fully anchored in the Self and capable of transmitting spiritual power to others.

Although she avoided such labels, Sally, at least in my eyes, was such a being.

In Dawn's recollection:

With Sally, you could feel the Shakti. You could feel the transmission, and that was the thread that pulled me in to study with her. It was very shamanic in that way. Sally would always say that Tantra—non-dual, spiritual tantric philosophy—is the closest yoga philosophy to shamanism. My meditation practice and deep dive into self-inquiry started with Pema Chödrön, a nun and scholar of Tibetan Buddhism. In 2010, I became deathly ill and was bedridden for eight months. Shortly after, I met a Siberian shaman who taught rituals to awaken the Divine Feminine and connect with the rhythms of the cosmos and the earth. These practices helped bring my vitality back.

Not long after, I met Sally, who for me was the bridge that connected the erudition of Pema with the life force energy of shamanic practices. Sally was an incredible scholar, with a massive amount of knowledge that backed up what she taught through deep lineage and texts like the Spanda Karikas, the Vijnana Bhairava, the Pratyabhijna Hrdayam, and many others. For so long, I didn't even know that she was drawing the meditations we practiced from those ancient scriptures. But at the same time, her emission of Shakti was palpable during those live classes and meditations. She was a shaman in the way that she transmitted the True Essence through the teleconferences.

And in Stephanie's:

And it was a very beautiful space in Brooklyn, and you know that because you studied with Sally: the Shakti would be so intense that you go into a sleep-like state, like a yoga nidra state, or a trance-like state, and and you're not trying to, it's just happening to you. It's what was coming through the field of energy that she held, like a wave taking over. And it was in one of these lucid, deep, transcendent states that her teacher appeared. Baba

Muktananda came by and bopped me on the head with a peacock feather. It was only late in the writing of our own stories for the forthcoming spiritual memoir "When She Wakes: Women's Stories of Kundalini Awakening" that I even remembered this, it was just in the last like six months, I'd totally forgotten about it.

And so, I mean, so you felt the power. You felt the lineage coming through her, right through her presence. It was unexpected, you know, you never knew when you showed up, what was going to unfold and happen. Eleven months before she passed away, I went to see her. I just wanted to be in the presence of my teacher, because I had studied with her for so many years. Living in South America, I wasn't in close physical proximity to her, but I was in the US for a period of time and was able to take advantage of the physicality to see her and be with her. It was the most wonderful moment to have a meal together, connect, laugh. It's something I now cherish and will forever.

SHAKTI AND THE DIVINE FEMININE

In addition to the gift of Shakti transmission, Sally was a pioneer in bringing the classic tantric teachings, mythology and yogic traditions into a modern western framing. She had the teacher's gift of making sophisticated and esoteric concepts accessible to even novice students. Her writings and scholarly interpretations are profound and prolific.

In Stephanie's words:

She was a master in her ability to speak and write and convey teachings. I guess that was very appealing to an intellectual mind like I have; there was good writing, like a good book that you're drawn to and you can't put it down, you don't want to put it down.

That's what Sally was to me, yeah, because there are other teachers that maybe say it in much more simple terms, like Thich Nath Than, I think he *was, you know, a master at simple ways to express deep truths. But Sally was like a good novel, a good, good historical novel, just so rich, you know, you just want to keep reading. You can't put it down because it's so damn good. So, there was that capacity to storytelling, in such a way that you're hooked.*

Her work on the power of the divine feminine, however, perhaps stands out the most—particularly given the era in which she began and the resistance she faced towards this kind of work. Born just a few generations after the infamous witchcraft trials in nearby Salem, Sally confidently proposed an even more radical idea: that the animating force of life was divine, that this power was feminine, and that for millennia, Indian mystics had learned to harness it for the transformation and evolution of human consciousness.

It was Sally's article on the Hindu Goddesses that first hooked me and have since created the foundations for my own teaching practice. She introduced me to the *Dasha Mahavidyas* (Ten Great Tantric Wisdom Goddesses), a group of powerful Shaktis who initiate and guide the Kundalini awakening process. They are not just abstract material forces but are living expressions of the flavors of reality that can be invoked through archetypal forms whose energy threads through different traditions.

Even for those unfamiliar with the yogic and tantric traditions, these goddesses dwell within our consciousness, ready to unveil their truths. They illuminate the immense power and love that underlie our reality and, most importantly, they inspire us to create this world anew. The deeper we connect with them, the more their fiery clarity strengthens us, and their ecstasy becomes our own.

In Dawn's words:

Deity yoga, Shakta Tantra and the teachings of the Goddess. The Shaktopaya is the main force of her teachings. Her ability to Awaken the Shakti life force within was her gift, and it is the main thread that's continuing to ripple out into the world.

Sally did not invent a new religion or philosophy; she harnessed thousands of years of study and adapted it for a Western audience, using language and conceptual frameworks that could be easily digested and built upon. Yet, like peer-reviewed science, her work was meticulously connected and traceable to the various lineages from which it emerged.

Her work is the voice of the goddess; a vision of the cosmos brimming with Her glory, rooted in the most ancient of scriptural soils, rejuvenated and enriched, eagerly awaiting the next generation to carry the fire.

Adore each being as me. I am you.

HUMILITY & DEVOTION

I have been blessed to have been studying at the feet of several great spiritual teachers over the past 30 years and each of them had a distinct style and approach. In reminiscing with fellow students about Sally, what stands out for me was her humility and devotion.

Sally had the ability to ground divinity in everyday human experience, making all who came to her feel worthy of her love and attention.

Transcript from my conversation with Stephanie:

Sundari Ma: For me, when I reflect on her life and what I received, it truly feels as if she embodied the Goddess Bhuvaneshvari so strongly. To me, her presence was the Heart—a vastness of space in which everything was welcome. I remember a line from a prayer that she liked to recite at the beginning of a class, after the invocation:

We ask that the great power of conscious evolution, the energy of awakening, touch all beings and draw us steadily to the recognition of our interconnectedness.

We ask that we know from within the absolute equality of all that lives.

Sundari Ma: This is what I always felt in her presence—the heart space. The heart where everything and everyone has a place. When personal issues came up for her or had been coming up in her own process, she would share them in such a humble way. She spoke about her own mistakes—those moments when she felt she had lost it or felt lost.

Stephanie: And that's unique to her as a teacher—to reveal those hiccups, those vulnerabilities, and not present a facade of ultimate perfection. I don't know many other teachers... I can't think of any right now who do that—those I've been exposed to, you know, who are willing to show their shortcomings.

Sundari Ma: Yes, it was very unique that she didn't want to be in the role of a guru. What she communicated—at least this is how it felt to me—was that she is one of us, with us on the path. Maybe like an Elder Sister, both in terms of her age and her experience. She was there to show and teach us what she knew and what she had discovered, all in this humble way.

Sally taught for over 40 years. Her devotion, her work ethic, the sheer volume of her work and the energy with which she applied herself suggests to me today something beyond just a commitment to the duties and responsibilities of being a spiritual teacher. In hearing Dawn share about her final course on karma, it struck me that there was a sense of urgency driving it all.

Not only could Sally feel intensely the shared suffering in our era, but she could connect with some of the growing dangers that threaten us today. She knew the only path forward was indeed an evolutionary one.

Dawn's memory of Sally's last lecture:

One month before her passing, Sally was pouring out her knowledge from a deep source connection, sharing esoteric and momentous teachings. She told us, 'You don't need to wait—just absorb these ancient teachings and knowledge.' It was as if she was urging us, 'You need to absorb and share this, get it out into the world. This is the time, and the planet needs it right now.'

During this final lecture, she had to be on oxygen the entire time, and at one point, she had to stop due to profuse coughing. She couldn't... we almost ended the class. It was her second lecture, and she was incredibly sick, barely able to continue. But she stayed—this was her Svadharma. She was meant to share and pass down this ancient wisdom until the very end.

That was in June 2023, and she passed away on July 10, 2023. Sally remains present through all her students, and her legacy continues through us. A deep bow of gratitude to the Universe for manifesting such an auspiciously beautiful soul.

RISE OF THE HOUSEHOLDER

It is worth taking a step back and examining the context of Sally's life and work.

Sally Kempton was born in Manhattan, New York in 1943. Shortly after Oppenheimer and his team began their work on unleashing the awesome power of nuclear fission. As though a direct divine rebuttal to the Manhattan project, Sally's life's work would become about unleashing the even more awesome power of Shakti into the modern world.

Though the link might not be immediately obvious, consider the possibility that if the 20th century is remembered for the scientific and industrial revolutions that yielded immense power, the 21st century must be the one that fosters the immense compassion and wisdom needed to tame that power.

Otherwise, there may not be a 22nd century.

And the awakened Shakti is that taming power. Once this inner fire is kindled, it does its work. It expands within as the light of consciousness, radiating outward from all who are baptized by this divine energy. Like Oppenheimer's fission reaction, each atomic awakening goes on to touch many more.

Kundalini awakening is an energetic process of transformation that occurs outside of the confines of language, within tradition or beyond it, and is agnostic of faith, creed, race, nationality, or temperament. The universality of Love awakening to itself initiates an irreversible and unstoppable chain reaction.

For thousands of years in spiritual communities, these deeper awakenings and more potent teachings were reserved for those deep inside the monastic life. Those on the "householder path" with careers and family had to settle for the faint echoes of the saints and great teachers who have graced this world.

Sally's work has completely reversed this paradigm. Not only is the householder's awakening enriching for the individual, but it is also the most vital next phase for the evolution of life today. The great scientific and industrial power unleashed in the 20th century can only be tamed and safeguarded in the 21st century through the awakening of those currently engaged in the worlds of science and industry.

The ashram is moving just down the hall from the boardroom and the lab.

It will be the awakened CEOs and investment bankers, teachers and army generals, scientists and politicians that bring harmony between great power and great wisdom, and even greater compassion.

Sally's work, based on heart-transmission and the awakening of Shakti, rooted in tradition, is a leap forward in the evolution of human consciousness. One that promises to help us navigate these delicate and volatile times with a little more grace, a little less enmity and a lot more love.

SUSTAINER OF WORLDS

A dear friend of mine recently shared an old hermetic text with me: Thoth's prophecy. It is a poetic lament about a world devoid of devotion.

Darkness will be preferred to light, and death will be thought more profitable than life; no one will raise his eyes to heaven; the pious will be deemed insane, and the impious wise; the madman will be thought a brave man, and the wicked will be esteemed as good. As for the soul, and the belief that it is immortal by nature, or may hope to attain immortality, as I have taught you, all this they will mock and will even persuade themselves that it is false. No word of reverence or piety, no utterance worthy of heaven will be heard or believed.

I think of Sally's work in the context of the world she entered in 1943 and the one she left behind in 2023. She was indeed a pious woman, and perhaps also deemed 'insane' by many around her for leaving a career in journalism, for following a *guru* of all people, and for moving to India of all places. Even for the greats, the spiritual path is not without its moments of doubt and despair.

A lone woman from New York, walking tall, headlong into a raging storm of indignity and suffering; noblesse unwavering because beneath the dignity and grace, the warmth and wisdom could only be the fiercest of wills. The kind of indomitable spirit and unfaltering faith needed to persevere through the most demanding of challenges. Pioneering qualities that have inspired and paved the way for this next generation to carry her work.

After nearly 30 years as a student at the feet of my teachers, I fully embraced my role and dharma as a teacher to share the knowledge and grace just a few months ago. I spoke to the owner of a yoga studio in Dubai about offering a weekend course on the divine feminine. Her first question to me was, *Have you ever heard of Sally Kempton?*

I could only smile with delight at the coincidence.

Sally's work lives on through Stephanie, Dawn, me, and so many others, carrying the seeds of her awakening power around the world. It is far too early to speak of her legacy, as the vibrancy of her teaching, the grace, and the reach of the Shakti are only just beginning to flourish. We can only look forward with anticipation to the fruits that will arise from Sally's life and imagine with delight the wonders this next generation, blessed and empowered by Shakti, will bestow upon the world.

"Now, I am become death, destroyer of worlds," He said.

"Now, I am become Love, sustainer of worlds," She answered.

-Sundari Ma

This is Tantra

The Tao of Anandamayi Ma

The heart that gives, gathers

"Although many stories have been shared about the miraculous happenings around her, it was the pure simplicity of her being that is the only miracle that strikes me today. Her surrender was so complete that she had become the valley through which the stream of grace moved effortlessly. She saw the Divine in everything and in everyone at all times. She would sit in silent ecstatic rapture for hours, completely absorbed in the One, her eyes glistening with the sweetness of the unseen."

A young woman came into my life recently, eager to know more about Tantra and the spiritual life in general. Her curious yet cautious approach reminded me of the very early days of my own journey. At the time, I had just begun taking a course on the Tao Te Ching and had stumbled on a book about the Indian Saint, Anandamayi Ma.

Learning about Lao Tzu and the Tao gently introduced me to a new way of looking at the world. A way of looking deeper, not just at life, but at the motion of life. Like how the vaporous white tops of the sea swell point at the unseen forces of wind and tide. The constant rhythm of wind and tide, hinting at something deeper still, in the movements of sun and moon, and so on.

But if the Tao was a gentle introduction to a new way of perceiving the world, discovering Anandamayi Ma for the first time revealed a radical new way of *being* in the world.

At first, it was her raw, magnetic beauty that pulled me in. The photos of her were mesmerizing, suggesting a quiet ecstasy and hinting at a connection with something that, at the time, was a great mystery to me. A new unseen force entered my life.

Many of her close disciples collected stories and paid tribute to all the stages of her life and her luminous presence. I remember reading as much as I could about her.

She claimed not to be a teacher, yet her teachings resound to this day. She claimed not to be a guru, yet some heads of state considered themselves her lifelong devotees. People flocked to her from every corner of the world; scholars, seekers, householders, and ascetics, all drawn by an invisible pull. They came burdened with questions, sorrows, and longings, and in her presence, those burdens melted away, not because she answered their questions, but because she *became* the answer.

In the words of Swami Sivananda, founder of the Divine Life Society of Rishikesh, Anandamayi Ma was the purest flower the soil of India has ever produced.

Like many other female Indian saints, she seemed to stand on the edge of several religious traditions, and in the midst of none. She did not teach in the conventional way but spoke with the authority of direct experience; she did not establish a doctrine, nor did she demand anything from her devotees.

Ram Dass summarized Anandamayi Ma's teachings beautifully:

Life and religion are one. All that you do to maintain your life, your everyday work and play, all your attempts to earn a living, should be done with sincerity, love and devotion, with a firm conviction that true living means virtually perfecting one's spiritual existence in tune with the universe. To bring about this synthesis, religious culture should be made as natural and easy as taking our food and drink when we are hungry and thirsty.

Her gatherings, according to those who witnessed them, were not orchestrated or rigidly planned; they simply *happened*. People were drawn to her, sitting at her feet for hours, sometimes in laughter, sometimes in tears, sometimes in silent awe or in a deep state of absorption. She fed them all; not only with food but with love, with stillness, with the simple touch of her gaze. When asked why so many came to her, she simply said, *They are all my own.*

Those near her experienced her presence as the ever-giving power of nature itself, like a river that never runs dry, never claiming anything. Those who came empty were filled; those who came full were emptied of illusion. And in this endless exchange of giving and receiving, Anandamayi Ma remained ever the same: overflowing yet untouched, offering all yet holding nothing.

She welcomed all with the openness of the sky, allowing them to find their own path through the light of her presence. This, the absolute light of understanding, shining upon all who came to her; *I see you dear. I feel your fear and anxiety and I love you all the more for it. I sense your frustration and despair and love you all the more for it. Let go now child and let my peace reign in your weary heart.*

Although many stories have been shared about the miraculous happenings around her, it was the pure simplicity of her being that is the only miracle that strikes me today. Her surrender was so complete that she had become the valley through which the stream of grace moved effortlessly. She saw the Divine in everything and in everyone at all times. She would sit in silent ecstatic rapture for hours, completely absorbed in the One, her eyes glistening with the sweetness of the unseen.

She was known for laughing often, as if she knew a secret the world had forgotten. And despite her wisdom, she carried the innocence and wonder of a child who has never left the garden of the cosmic play. She had nothing to attain, no mission to accomplish, no kingdom to build. She was simply awake. She lived, and in living, she revealed.

He alone is, she would say. Whether you worship Christ, Krishna, Kālī or Allah, you actually worship the one Light that is also in you, since It pervades all things.

This is the Tao of Anandamayi Ma. It is the Tao of Neem Karoli Baba. And it is the Tao of St-Francis, Siddhi Ma and every great saint who has ever walked among us. It is the way of Grace and does not require a head full of teachings but rather a heart full of faith and courage; to surrender so absolutely that which is most precious to that which is most ineffable. And in that surrender, a wellspring of love and devotion gushes forth.

The way of Grace is not a path to be followed, nor is it an admonishment for those on a different path or none at all. There's no chiding here, no call to action or strive with greater intensity. The way of Grace demands nothing and offers everything.

Anandamayi Ma is a blessing from on high, Grace's exultation, an effervescent and fragrant reminder that we, are loved. That each and every one of us is held in the great heart of all hearts, always and forever.

In Anandamayi Ma's cosmic playground, no child is less worthy of a mother's love than any other. In this playground, we work and play, we marry and we mourn, sometimes stumbling, and sometimes hurting a little too much. And when that moment finally arrives, when we find ourselves in the depths of anguish and sorrowful confusion, the slightest turn towards the light is enough. Grace comes rushing forth, like a father towards his lost daughter or a mother towards her prodigal son.

Like the many saints before her and those yet to come, Anandamayi Ma is a beacon, forever lighting the way home. And just as the vaporous white tops of a sea swell hint at the unseen forces of wind, tide, sun and moon, Anandamayi Ma points us so exquisitely toward the ineffable Grace behind all things.

In her words:

Whether you know it or not, I am your nearest and dearest - your very own Self.

Your sorrow, your pain, your agony is indeed my sorrow. This body understands everything.

When by the flood of your tears, the inner and the outer have fused into one, you will find Her whom you sought with such anguish, nearer than the nearest, the very breath of life, the very core of every heart.

If you cannot do anything else, at least morning and evening at the appointed time, lay down your body, mind, and life before Him in salutation and surrender, and think of Him just a little.

So this is my only request to you: to make a place for me in your hearts.

This is Tantra

The Knowledge that Liberates and the Teacher Who Set Me Free

•

A love letter to Igor Kufayev and the teachers who carry the sacred fire

"Like so many students before me who have been guided along this path, I was afraid of surrendering completely; of touching this place of total trust in the one guiding me. Only to find that, somehow, through the miracle of it all, there are people who walk this earth who want for nothing and give themselves fully to this work."

In Tantra, the *teacher* holds a unique role. More than passing down knowledge, they embody it. They carry the blazing light of the Self and ignite it in others. When we are struck by this lightning bolt of recognition, a reverse process begins. *The Word*, a deeper, untouchable Knowledge emerges: one beyond intellect, beyond words, beyond personality. It cannot be spoken. It is knowing itself.

Grace can enter in many ways, but traditionally, it was the enlightened teacher who bestowed it, piercing the shell of our contracted state and offering everything we needed to grow into the maturity of being both, fully human and divine, liberated whilst in this body - *jīvanmukta*.

I consider myself blessed beyond measure to have had extraordinary teachers in my life. In addition to Sally Kempton, I'd like to encourage anyone reading to seek out the work of Dr. David Frawley, Yogini Shambhavi and Igor Kufayev.

Each one unique, yet all dedicated to upholding dharma and serving humanity through a time, when for many, the deepest of truths are buried under a mountain of deceptions.

DR. DAVID FRAWLEY

I once stood beside Dr. Frawley in the crisp air of the Himalayas of Uttarakhand. His gaze fixed on the sacred Trishul mountain in the distance. But it wasn't the mountain that held my attention, it was the complete and utter devotion I sensed in Dr. Frawley in that moment. It wasn't just another pilgrimage. I felt his *love* for this mountain as if he was reuniting with a long lost old friend.

Dr. Frawley taught me reverence, like a father teaching a daughter. The vastness of Dr. Frawley's Vedic scholarship only hints at the love held within his heart for the sacred sites and all that helps to liberate a person, especially the ancient seers who devoted their lives to

Perennial Wisdom and leaving a trail for others to follow.

Throughout all of his work, the attentive student can feel echoes of the hymns of the *rishis* who composed the Rig Veda thousands of years ago.

Dr. Frawley's three books on mantra and inner tantric yoga that have been my close companions for the past 15 years. To this day, these books continue to reveal finer and finer layers of wisdom.

For many, Dr. Frawley is one of the most brilliant Vedic scholars of our age but for me he is the great swan, *Paramahaṃsa*, a being who freely navigates the heavens of the immortal Self, and I am so deeply grateful to have been his student.

YOGINI SHAMBHAVI

I was nervous about meeting Yogini Shambhavi for the first time. I had seen photos of this beautiful woman and heard of her immense spiritual power. Upon meeting Shambhavi however, everything shifted inside me instantly. Her adoration for the Divine Mother radiated palpably and pulled me into a feeling of love so intimate and so very sweet.

I had longed to be initiated into tantric sādhana and receive the mantras of the Goddess. Without hesitation, she took my hand and led me into that sacred space.

Her guidance didn't stop there. Shambhavi showed me how joy can unfold in the simplest of moments on the path of Shakti; preparing Mung Dhal the way it was cooked in her family; how to wrap a sari, and how to move with grace, strength and playfulness as a woman.

It was Yogini Shambhavi who brought me to ancient Devi and Shiva temples tucked deep in the Himalayas, where I could receive their blessings. And through her I learned to feel the magic that vibrates throughout life; how each plant, each animal, every mountain and tree carries the unique signature of the Mother Goddess; each a conscious act of love and creation deserving the highest admiration and reverence.

IGOR VAMADEVA KUFAYEV

And finally, what to say about the man who set me free?

For many, Igor is a public figure. His *darshans* are freely available on the internet. Igor is an originating source, a fountainhead; for those with ears to hear, Igor's voice echoes of thunder in the valley. And for those with hearts to feel, the power of the Word echoes in the heart of an artist and lover of humanity; his collection of works are a font of love and wisdom that will be treasured by future generations.

For me however, Igor is not a public figure at all but indeed a very personal one. It has been my life's honor to serve in Igor's sangha and learn the art of spiritual alchemy at the feet of a true master.

It was only *behind the scenes* however, where I could feel the depths of Igor's love and compassion. Tender and unexpected moments of generosity and warmth. It was when nobody else was looking that I could witness the personal sacrifices, big and small. And most of all, I feel the deepest of admiration towards Igor's courage and strength, he stands unwavering on the rock of ages as though sculpted from it.

He once asked me what I feared most about the student-teacher relationship. He knew the answer, he just wanted to make sure I did too.

I was afraid of losing myself in love.

Like so many students before me who have been guided along this path, I was afraid of surrendering completely; of touching this place of total trust in the one guiding me. Only to find that, somehow, through the miracle of it all, there are people who walk this earth who want for nothing and give themselves fully to *this work*.

In the words of Kahlil Gibran: *And there are those who give and know not pain in giving, nor do they seek joy, nor give with mindfulness of virtue; They give as in yonder valley the myrtle breathes its fragrance into space. Through the hands of such as these God speaks, and from behind their eyes. He smiles upon the earth.*

Igor guided me beyond what I had known and believed myself to be, beyond any outer rituals or conceptual understanding. He showed me the ancient way in which the knowledge of the Self has been passed down through the ages; like a chain of light, heart to heart. He nurtured me, tested me, and helped me stand on my own. And in the end, he set me free.

And how to say thank you to the man who set me free?

How to say thank you to Sally, Dr. Frawley and Yogini Shambhavi who gave me so much and asked for so little?

How to thank Grace with anything less than all that I am.

From generation to generation, the Word is preserved and from heart to heart, it is enriched and enlivened. Today, I write with a weepy gratitude for the old man and woman in black, sitting under the night sky by the eternal campfire, eagerly awaiting their daughters' and sons' safe journey back home.

In the end is the Word, and the Word is with God, and the Word is God.

A U M

-Sundwari Ma

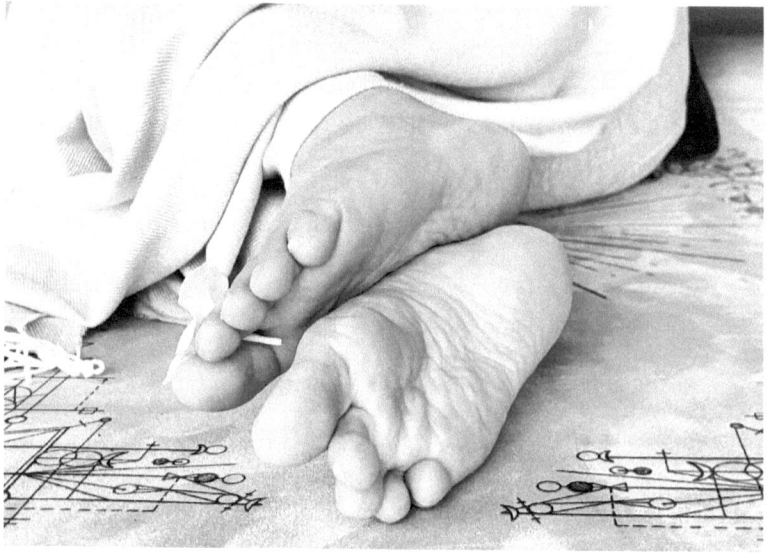

Selected Essays & Reflections

IMMERSIONS

&

TRANSFORMATIONS

This is Tantra

From the Mountain Top to the Valley

·

Lessons in Humility and Living Truth

"Imagine how I felt after seeing him that weekend, that shift in his heart and the light of peace and wonder radiating from his eyes.

What's the appropriate way of thanking you for that? Which section of the greeting card store should I look in? You said it was Grace, right? How could I thank Grace with anything less than all that I am."

In this article and podcast I explore recent work around connecting Tantric Meditation with 12th-Step Recovery Programs. The experience is still very fresh, remarkable, and, frankly, humbling. The desire to somehow fit it all neatly into a satisfying intellectual framing has been resisted and instead, dear reader, I leave you simply with the rawness of my own experience, more or less as it unfolded.

ZOOM AND POTATO CHIPS;

Oh dear Lord, you are really going to make me an instrument...

It's hard for me to believe my life could be transformed so dramatically from a single video session less than a year ago. Especially since I am usually the one on these calls facilitating transformation in others.

In my previous role as a *spiritual facilitator* I had assisted many people with their awakening process. I have heard many stories and challenges, helped people break through various forms of resistance or deal with unexpected obstacles. This call would be different.

The man was calling me about potato chips.

I had met him before briefly on a meditation immersion. I was surprised when he booked a session with me. If I'm honest, I even felt a little insecurity. The man had a certain presence about him. Successful in business, a long time spiritual practitioner and family man. I couldn't imagine what possible problem he could have that I could help with.

He joined the Zoom call from a café in Dubai. A huge plant with dark green leaves stood beside him. He was smiling and had an easy carefree charm when he greeted me.

We exchanged pleasantries and updates about the recent immersion where we had met before he finally got into the reason for his call.

I'm really struggling with potato chips. Every night. I eat a bag, sometimes two.

I didn't believe him.

Or more specifically, I believed that he may have indeed struggled with junk food like so many of us do, I just didn't believe that this was why he called.

And though I had never addressed the topic of potato chips with anyone before, I tried to approach the problem as professionally as possible, even if I felt a bit awkward. I spoke at length about the origins of food cravings, the six tastes in Ayurveda, and even plum chutney recipes.

He thanked me and seemed quite satisfied by my response. Ten minutes of a ninety minute session had elapsed and I waited with anticipation to hear what this call would really be about.

His smile turned into a mischievous grin.

Maybe a little more background then. Before the potato chips, I used to drink too much. Have you ever heard of Alcoholics Anonymous?

But instead of continuing down the line of his own journey, the man began to share passionately about his AA community. Eventually it became clear that he did not come to the meditation immersion for himself and this call wasn't going to be about him. He wanted to know if Tantra could facilitate spiritual awakenings in AA.

His eyes began to glow and I was being absorbed into his love for his tribe as he called it.

He explained that people who joined AA in fact relied on a spiritual awakening as a means of recovering from a debilitating and destructive affliction.

I think what you are doing, this Tantra thing—Kundalini and all that—I think it's what the AA founders were looking for; it's the missing piece. It's Grace at the level of experience, not in a textbook.

The now famous '12 Steps' promise a spiritual awakening and they do deliver on that but for most people, it's a mild psychological awakening. It's tenuous, vulnerable-like.

One of the founders, Bill W experienced the full awakening. The white light, holy shit, descending-grace-my-pants-are-on-fire-moment. That incandescent, irreversible and irrevocable moment where everything changes. But it's so rare!

One of those steps (Step 11) addresses prayer and meditation. It's the least practiced step in AA, probably because so few people really believe there is actual raw power that can be tapped, let alone how they might go about connecting with it.

If people in AA or any of the other 12-Step Programs knew about your kind of tantric meditation it would impact the world and I'm not joking. Millions of people are in anonymous 12-Step Programs and millions more qualify. Doctors, lawyers, politicians, vagabonds and erstwhile free spirits all sharing the same space, same steps, same principles, looking for that spiritual awakening.

All these people suffering from addiction, these are your seekers. This is the West's missing Brahmin class. They are your future mystics and poets, saints and teachers. They've just been soothing their deep longing for the divine with Johnny Walker and Percocet. You connect the 11th step with Tantra and you will light a fire in the heart of every major city and community on this planet.

I knew little about AA or twelve-steps programs. The man's enthusiasm was contagious but it wasn't yet clear to me what he wanted or how I could help.

I steered the conversation back towards him and his awakening process. And this is when it struck me. So many of these calls with me were about *the process*. The ways and means of the expansion of consciousness. Kundalini, Shakti, Prana and none of this was of interest to him. He seemed to have no interest in himself whatsoever.

The call reverberated with me for weeks.

Something about the way he spoke. The warmth and goodwill that seemed to flow so effortlessly. He oozed humility and tender compassion. It wasn't the innocent compassion of a child but the rich compassion of a man who had travelled the world and made peace with its dark crevices.

My whole adult life I had been studying at the feet of great teachers and here was this man teaching me something. A man who by his own admission simply prayed like a child, on his knees every morning, hands clasped together on the side of his bed, praying to be of maximum service to God and his fellow man.

It was as though St-Francis himself stopped in front of my yogini cave and waved, *follow me down into the valley below.*

The intense devotion this man felt began to stir something in me, giving rise to waves of fear; the kind that is sparked when the body intuits that change is coming. I had spent the last nine years volunteering for a spiritual organization. My body knew, even before the rest of me did, that soon I'd be on a flight to Dubai, stepping out on my own without the security of an established organization and teacher behind me.

CIGARETTES AND SAMADHI;
Where there is injury, pardon. Where there is doubt, faith.

I imagine that, for any teacher, there is this moment – the first hour of the first day of the first school year. Looking out at the young students in the classroom, eager children beginning to quieten, their gaze shifting in anticipation to the eyes of the teacher who fondly looks back. The cooling Fall air outside, while inside, the stillness of that moment, vibrant and fertile with the possibility of what might unfold.

When my first moment as a spiritual teacher came, it wasn't in a classroom but a suburban yoga studio in Dubai. The air outside didn't carry the scent of early fall back home; instead, it was so hot it singed the nostrils. And the room full of students were not in fact children but, as my friend had referred to his 12-step community, *Vikings*.

This is not going to be your regular spiritual community experience. When you meet them, know that these are Vikings. Warriors, wounded maybe, but everyone in that room got there because they are strong. Until the awakening happens, addiction is a daily battle that for many lasted decades.

Every AA meeting is basically a group of strangers gathering together to work on their virtues; to build their character. There are no teachers, no leaders. No real rules or authority of any kind except for a few traditions. There's an ongoing joke in the rooms that AA works because we are never all crazy at the same time. As in any given moment there is someone deeply sane in the meeting and that person becomes the teacher for the day.

What you end up with is a lot of raw honesty and a level of integrity that you won't find in many other places. It's no frills, no bullshit, all-action spiritual work, so bring your most authentic self and whatever you do, don't lead off with a sing song. Also go easy on the Sanskrit.

The room was dimly lit and had heavy beige theater-style curtains in front of the big windows. Yoga straps were hanging from the ceiling and the blanks of the wooden floor had become loose over the years. The AC was pretty noisy but turning it down would transform the space into a sauna in no time. It was 47 °C outside. But the setting and details of it didn't really matter to me. What mattered was that I was here now. I felt excitement, anticipation, slight nervousness and a strong surge of energy in my body, as if an ocean wave wanted to break at the shore. My mind was getting blank. There was nothing to hold on to anymore. Something else was in charge now.

I sat cross legged on a blanket across from a man in a t-shirt. He emptied his pockets beside him and out came an iPhone, car keys and a packet of red Marlboros. He smiled and I smiled back. The room had filled up and there was no discernible pattern. Ages ranged from early twenties to mid-fifties, men and women alike.

They had organized together to gather the funds and bring me to Dubai for a weekend. They had showed up that day with anticipation and enthusiasm. They knew nothing about me or tantric meditation, they had simply been told I could help them connect with a God of their understanding. That was all it took.

As I looked across the room and met each one in their eyes, I could feel the intensity of their longing, the sincerity of their devotion and the gentleness of their hearts.

I have heard all kinds of theories on alcoholism and addiction over the years, but never one that seemed to truly get at the nature of my experience. But if I had to pick, it's what Carl Jung intimated in his '61 letter to Bill Wilson. That the craving for alcohol is actually a spiritual thirst, a yearning for divine union. An elegant way of saying we were looking for Love in all the wrong places.

Said differently, if the Dalai Llama or Shri Ramana would have been born in the one tavern town I grew up in, they'd probably have found their way to AA too.

Understand though, for people in AA the yearning is some passing fancy, like wanting a new car, it's a life-defining burning desire that won't be truly satiated until that union is realized. It's all about the intensity and I think you will feel that in the room.

As I began the work of guiding the room into meditation, the man with the Marlboros began to tremble and shake. This astonished me.

Of course I have seen this kind of involuntary physical manifestation at so many past immersions but almost never so quickly and with someone so new to the practice.

Before long, the entire room had gone. Despite most of the group being new to meditation, every single person was in varying degrees of samadhi. The air in the room had become heavy and the silence was thick. A few people began displays of spontaneous movements but mostly it was the kind of deep, refined silence I had only ever experienced with very advanced tantric practitioners.

Even writing about this now, it's hard for me to grasp how truly remarkable this is. A room full of non-meditators going into samadhi and some of them piercing the deepest inner layers; and not in some Himalayan cave but in the Dubai suburbs. It was truly an astounding moment to witness and partake in.

Yeah I remember that weekend. The red Marlboros on the floor and yes I was surprised. I was hoping that at least five or six people out of the fifteen or so would have that aha moment.

I couldn't believe it. I think everyone except for one or two experienced something profound. When it was over and everyone left, I got a little weepy just thinking about how everyone looked by the second day. Wide-eyed stares, innocent and full of wonder.

You made them believe in magic again and what more noble goal of spiritual work could there be than the restoration of awe and wonder at the heart of creation.

This is just the beginning.

GRIT AND GRACE;

For it is in giving that we receive...

Steven, who had participated in the first AA meditation weekend, generously offered to support me during my time in Dubai; driving me around, helping with errands, and sharing his favorite finds. He introduced me to the best organic coconut water, and passed along the contact of a local farmer who delivered homemade ghee, fresh eggs, and organic milk. He chauffeured me to the ocean, helped to organize my events, and even picked up a harmonium from the other side of town. As we crisscrossed the highways of the city, he began sharing his story with a level of honesty, rawness, and sincerity that was both rare and humbling.

Here was a man, 43 years old, who had been wrestling with alcohol addiction for the past two decades. Twenty-two years of carrying shame, guilt, anger, and hopelessness; of clawing his way out of the swamp only to find himself slipping back in. It was a battle as relentless as it was raw, each day a blend of failure and courage, pushing through exhaustion and confusion and the ever-present lure of relief in the bottle.

Witnessing his transformation in the wake of our tantric meditation weekend over just a few weeks time is one of the great miracles of life I have been blessed to witness.

He began meditating twice a day with his AA sponsor, our mutual friend, while continuing with his twelve-step program. His face started to glow, not just from restful sleep, but as if his spirit was returning, his eyes reflecting a liveliness and joy he hadn't felt in years. For the first time, he slept peacefully curled up like a cat, feeling at ease in his own skin and in the company of others.

He found the courage to confront waves of anger and feelings of inadequacy. Gradually, he began to be of service to others in need, feeling the return of purpose and confidence. He was falling in love with his own life.

I have worked with a fair number of people over the years. Guiding them through the steps and what not. In AA we call that a sponsor and yes I sponsored Steven and yes, until you showed up, it was heartbreaking.

Because with some people they just work so desperately hard to reach this plateau of 'normal'. A level of normal that for everyone else is just a given; to wake up in the morning not wanting to kill yourself or to go to bed at night knowing which city you are in.

And Steven was doing everything right as far as this work goes, and we'd made a little bit of progress before suddenly it was like a wave just came over him and brought him out to sea. And there was nothing to be done with except walk lonely by the shoreline, praying and hoping that the ocean would cough him back up.

And when you do this sponsorship work, sometimes you fall in love. I mean for me, Steven is like a brother, we have gotten so close. Then it becomes so much harder when the wave comes. It's devastating, truly.

So that was my prayer for you, for him and everyone in the room that weekend. That somehow someway through the magic of this Tantra and whatever happens behind the scenes, the heavens would open and Grace would descend and touch Steven and everyone in that room.

You asked me once about my spiritual process and why I don't care to talk about it. But consider it now that you know what I feel about Steven.

Imagine how I felt after seeing him that weekend, that shift in his heart and the light of peace and wonder radiating from his eyes.

What's the appropriate way of thanking you for that? Which section of the greeting card store should I look in? You said it was Grace, right? How could I thank Grace with anything less than all that I am.

Back when I was agnostic to this whole spiritual scene, I heard an old man speak. He said, 'I have never seen the wind, but I have seen what the wind can do and I have never seen God but I have seen what God can do.'

You saw the miracle now with your own eyes. A life redeemed and restored. All the people he is now going to touch in his remaining years; friends, family, community, work... these miracles ripple through generations.

And this oh-so-loving animating power behind it all, and I get to take part in that process! I do this St-Francis prayer every day with all my heart and at least a few times per year, I get to participate in an honest to god miracle. For a moment, my ordinary life becomes something so rare and extraordinary and I feel intrinsically connected to an unbroken chain of goodness that stretches back to the very dawn of time.

I have never seen God, but I have seen what God can do and that's enough for me to go all in. What else is there to talk about after that?

When grace enters, everything is possible and Steven was more than ready to shake off the dark mantle he had worn for so long and allow his radiant heart to be revealed.

I'm so grateful that he agreed to share his story publicly through a podcast with me. So deeply grateful also to the man with the Marlboros and Steven's anonymous group of friends for their trust and goodwill.

And how to express my gratitude to the Grace behind all things with anything less than all that I am...

It is in dying that we are born to eternal life.

This is Tantra

Stille Nacht, Heilige Nacht

•

So hallow'd and so gracious is the time

"Out of such darkness stepped two men to try and soothe the broken-hearted. And if their life circumstances are hard for me to imagine, it is even more difficult to fathom the kind of resilience and faith needed for that night to unfold. At this, I can only wonder."

To all my dear friends who have known me for years and to those who have recently joined my Substack, I want to express my deep appreciation for your support.

December 24th has always been a magical day for me.

Growing up, this day marked a time of warmth and generosity of spirit. A day where I felt the power of community; where the essentials of the heart emerged, petty grievances were set aside and our shared humanity was remembered.

And by moment, only wonder…

SILENT NIGHT

The origin of this classic carol is not far from my hometown, and even closer to the farmhouse of my maternal grandparents.

On a cold Christmas Eve in 1818, Joseph Mohr walked the three kilometres from his home in Oberndorf near Salzburg to visit his friend Franz Xaver Gruber in the neighbouring town of Arnsdorf near Laufen. Mohr brought with him a poem he had written some two years earlier. He needed a carol for the Christmas Eve midnight Mass that was only a few hours away, and hoped his friend, a school teacher who also served as the church's choir master and organist, could set his poem to music. Gruber composed the melody for Mohr's "Stille Nacht" in just a few hours. - Wikipedia

It's hard for me today to imagine the circumstances that inspired Father Mohr. A town torn apart by the Napoleonic Wars, plagued by failed harvests, grief, despair, and misery. As the legend goes, Mohr found himself with neither a school nor a cemetery when he wrote his now-famous poem.

Out of such darkness stepped two men to try and soothe the broken-hearted. And if their life circumstances are hard for me to imagine, it is even more difficult to fathom the kind of resilience and faith needed for that night to unfold. At this, I can only wonder.

Decades later, the same carol echoed through the trenches of the Western Front. On Christmas Eve of 1914, amidst one of the most brutal and merciless conflicts in recorded history of war, over one hundred thousand men laid down their arms to sing this song to each other.

Such is the power that flowed through the hearts of Priester Mohr and Franz Xaver.

> *Stille Nacht, heilige Nacht,*
> *Alles schläft; einsam wacht*
> *Nur das traute, hochheilige Paar.*
> *Holder Knabe im lockigen Haar,*
> *Schlaf in himmlischer Ruh!*
> *Schlaf in himmlischer Ruh!*
>
> *Stille Nacht, heilige Nacht,*
> *Hirten erst kundgemacht*
> *Durch der Engel Halleluja,*
> *Tönt es laut von fern und nah:*
> *Christ, der Retter ist da!*
> *Christ, der Retter ist da!*
>
> *Stille Nacht, heilige Nacht,*
> *Gottes Sohn, o wie lacht*
> *Lieb' aus deinem göttlichen Mund,*
> *Da uns schlägt die rettende Stund'.*
> *Christ, in deiner Geburt!*
> *Christ, in deiner Geburt!*

ECHOES IN THE VALLEY

Some say that ever 'gainst that season comes Wherein our Saviour's birth is celebrated, This bird of dawning singeth all night long; And then, they say, no spirit dare stir abroad, The nights are wholesome, then no planets strike, No fairy takes, nor witch hath power to charm, So hallow'd and so gracious is the time. – Hamlet

The Holy Night, Christmas Eve, has always been my favorite celebration. Candles glowing warmly inside, the chill of winter lingering outside; the choir at our church and my mother's eyes, shining. A freshly cut fir tree, brought home by my grandfather, breathing the crisp scent of the forest into our living room.

My grandfather nurtured his Christmas trees all year long. His field, just above the main house at the forest's edge, was a wonderland of evergreen trees. Tall and short, some with deep green needles, others shimmering in blue or silver. I liked the trees with softer needles; they seemed gentler, more welcoming to a child's touch. Opa was meticulous in his care. To ensure the trees grew perfectly, he would collect stones of just the right size and weight, and hang them from uneven branches to correct and guide their shape. It was a delicate science, a labor of love, his form of devotion.

He was a strong man, a commanding figure with a voice that could fill the valley. He was deeply respected in the community and church, where he was an active member. On his walks through the forest, he sang hymns to Jesus with such gusto that I can still hear his voice echoing through the hills, carrying his spirit far and wide.

My younger brother and I couldn't help but giggle at his enthusiasm. At bedtime, his songs became softer, old German lullabies and gospel hymns, laced with humor as he replaced certain words to make us laugh.

In the farmhouse kitchen, my grandmother prepared for

Christmas with equal dedication. She filled large aluminium tins with an assortment of cookies she baked each year for all her grandchildren. My favorites were the jam-filled red currant cookies and the orange rounds drizzled with dark chocolate. The hallway, always cool, smelled faintly of butter and spices. Whenever I smell Christmas cookies, I'm transported back into the Christmas of my childhood.

My grandparents were Protestant Christians. It was my grandfather who taught me how to pray. Each night in bed after the lights have been switched off, I would close my eyes, fold my hands and talk to Jesus, sharing the joys and worries of my little world with him.

December 24th was a day like no other in our family. Anticipation filled the air. That morning, the Christmas tree was brought inside. My brother and I would decorate it with ornaments that carried years of memories. Small red apples, delicate straw stars, glass balls, wooden angels, sweets wrapped in foil, and real red candles, all of it transformed the tree into something magical. My mother's touch made it even more special; she used the same decorations year after year, as if each ornament held a fragment of our family's story.

By late afternoon, the busyness of the day quieted. We dressed in our finest clothes and set out for the church. Outside, the world was cloaked in darkness, but the houses along the way glowed with warm lights. Inside the church, wooden benches creaked softly as families gathered and filled the rows. The story of Bethlehem unfolded, retold year by year with reverence and wonder. The pipe organ's deep, resonant tones filled the air, and the congregation's voices rose together in prayer and gratitude.

In those moments, the burdens and grievances of the year were forgotten, forgiven, or just set aside for a night.

Together, we celebrated the birth of Jesus, the promise of hope, kindness and community. It was a night of reconnecting; with each other, with faith, and with something greater than ourselves.

After the mass, we lingered outside under a sky filled with stars, and sometimes a blanket of clouds. Families huddled together, exchanging wishes of *Frohe Weihnachten*. *Froh* is an old German word for happy but a happiness that is caused by an inner wave of serene delight.

This Christmas, this 24th of December, 2024, will be a particularly special night for me. After spending several months in the desert of Dubai, I will be coming home. It will be a time of reconnection and renewal.

I will give thanks on this Holy Night as I sit next to my mother in her favorite church, listening to the story of Bethlehem retold with reverence and wonder. I will give thanks as I eat Christmas cookies with my niece and nephew. I will give thanks as I step into my mother's garden at night, inhaling the crisp air and perhaps hearing the faint sounds of nature. I will give thanks to my friends, old and new. I will give thanks when eyes meet in silent acknowledgment of the preciousness of being together, of sharing a moment, sharing the breath, holding each other, and simply being alive.

I will give thanks to you, dear reader, for following me on this adventure into the heart of love and life. My words come alive only because you read them and this means so much to me. From the depths of my being, thank you.

May this night be filled with light and magic for you and your families; and with the warmth of the heart reaching those who need it.

With so much Love to you and yours,

Frohe Weihnachten!

Sundari Ma

Therein Lies the Peace of God

•

Prayer is better than sleep

"Those things we all fight for each and every day, that drive to survive and thrive along with it, fading into the still of this night. There is no doing on this tantric path. There is, simply, surrendering to the great seduction at the very core of all life, the longing to go home."

This thing you do... Tantra... all this spirituality and religion stuff... God, what's it all about?

I never imagined I would find myself living in the desert of the United Arab Emirates.

The community I moved into last month was built by four brothers who grew up in what was then Palestine. They modeled it after the village of their childhood; not just a neighborhood, but a true community.

There are stables within a short walk from every villa and apartment with a dozen or so horses, greenhouses with communal herb gardens, and a walking trail where free-roaming chickens, ducks and peacocks wander without rules.

There are two schools here, and on my morning walks, I watch as children can't resist feeding the animals or chasing the chickens, while their parents do their best to guide them back to the path before the morning bell.

At the heart of this community is a large open courtyard with six restaurants; Thai, Japanese, Mexican, Italian, Arabic and fusion. There's also a café beside a shop that only sells locally produced honey. After my walk through the gardens, I often find myself sipping a latte on the café terrace, watching how the light turns the shop window amber and gold.

None of the restaurants serve alcohol, and somehow, this makes it clearer that this courtyard belongs to the children. On weekends, from morning until late at night, the air fills with their play and laughter; interrupted only by the sounds from the nearby Mosque.

Come to prayer... come to prayer...

Friday is the mosques' busiest day. Worshipers from outside the community arrive, red and white cones are set up to create extra parking. The mosque overflows, and so outside, in the shade of trees and along sidewalks, strangers kneel together on prayer mats, foreheads touching the ground in unison.

They come to prayer. And when they leave, always, seeming to walk a beat slower. Their gait, a little lighter, as though the air itself has turned more tender and more merciful.

Also in the courtyard is the yoga studio where I hold the tantric meditations. On Friday nights, I hold space for a small group of people, most of whom are only beginning their inner journey.

While holding space is always a blessing for me, there's something particularly special about witnessing someone meditate for the first time and experiencing some of the deepest inner states; their utter astonishment and delight at discovering what is available to all of us.

One of my students made a joke the other night of how good my job was; of all the kinds of work a person could do in this world, mine was like giving out free ice cream to children.

And yes, sometimes, it feels that way. At other times, it is harrowing. Those who have experienced tragedy, buried pain, deep enmity; all this suffering must be faced before it can be released. This is the work. And free ice cream.

And then, on the rarest of occasions, the work is simply sacred, in the purest sense of the word.

On those nights, I simply bear witness with heart agape.

This past Friday night was one such occasion.

It wasn't a burning bush. No one was miraculously healed, no one levitated or spoke in tongues.

It was something far simpler and pedestrian and yet still caused me to hold back tears.

Seven of us sat in a circle on the wooden floor of the courtyard yoga studio. A few flower petals had been placed at the head of everyone's mat. The room was dimly lit. The air carried the scent of earthy incense while the sound of children playing flowed in from the courtyard.

In front of me, a harmonium and my travel alter; a small embroidered fabric with cherished images.

I had finished the invocation and guided the group into meditation.

I watched on as everyone descended deeper into the silence. For some, the gentlest of flowing movements began. For others, the softest of smiles. Faces becoming ageless, skin beginning to shine.

In these moments it sometimes happens that people experience spontaneous movements or sudden sounds as the journey into peace touches points of catharsis. But not on this night. The peace only got deeper for everyone, including me. The pull was getting ever stronger, the will to resist dissolving like a sandcastle into the waves.

Each breath became ever subtler, receding and withdrawing to its source.

Those things we all fight for each and every day, that drive to survive and thrive along with it, fading into the still of this night. There is no doing on this tantric path. There is, simply, surrendering to the great seduction at the very core of all life, the longing to go home.

Then, the prayer from the mosque began pouring into the space.

It was the first night of Ramadan; *the night of power*

Every land carries its own vibration. It's not just the landscape that shapes a country's essence; it's the traditions of its people, the resonance of their values, the sound of their heart beats, the frequency of their traditional food, and maybe most of all, the energy of their prayers.

For a brief moment on Friday night, it was as though the entire desert outside swelled with divine love. And in that moment, the mosque became something else for me. A bastion of love and light, holding the children in the courtyard and the adults in the studio in its protective embrace.

Inside the room, I watched as the people in front of me fell into the deepest state of silence possible, while what felt like wave after wave of ethereal goodness moved through the room.

Later, after guiding everyone back and resting, some people shared about their experience.

I felt waves of peace coming at me, another man added. It was like waves were washing away year after year of old tensions. I remember at one point thinking, oh… there goes 2006!

But mostly we sat in comfortable silence together. Until the moment that moved me to tears.

A man began to speak who had been coming regularly. He recently started bringing a friend to the gatherings. This was a friend he cared deeply for; and when he spoke softly, his voice quivered with devotion and gratitude. He looked at his friend's face, pointing at him awkwardly and offering shyly:

Therein lies the peace of God.

And indeed, his friend was *lit from within*. His skin glowed in its softness, his smile warm and effortless, and his tender heart radiating the peace of that which is eternal.

A peace that does not mark the absence of conflict but rather the absolute ground of being itself. The peace from which all things arise and to which all things return.

The friend had come to a courtyard yoga studio for a simple end-of-the-week meditation, only to get swept away in the currents of worship echoing from the mosque, on a holy night. Then finding himself washed on to the shores of the infinite, his mind not yet able to comprehend the magnitude of this unfolding.

I didn't want to come out, he said. *I wanted to stay there*, he said.

It happens like this sometimes in tantric meditation. The ocean currents of consciousness coalesce just so. The moon and the planets align in exactly the right way. The mosque begins its prayers at exactly the right time. And the fraternal love and prayers of a single man profoundly impacting the heart of another.

Come to prayer… come to prayer…

It is not the kind of life-saving miracle that will make the day's headlines.

But one that is now etched in my heart.

This oh-so-ordinary miracle of love. One person, caring so passionately about the wellbeing of another. A man, becoming lit from within on the first night of Ramadan to the sounds of prayer on an otherwise typical Friday night in a Palestinian-inspired village in the middle of the desert, complete with a sushi bar and free-roaming peacocks.

To all my Muslim friends, Ramadan Mubarak!

Man vs the Goddess

•

Alone, we never stood a chance.

"*It was a glorious defeat; he went out on his shield, as the saying goes. I admired him for trying, truly. But let's be honest here: my dear friend was attempting to resist the power of the Goddesses. What exactly did he think was going to happen!?*"

Sons of Rudra and Daughters of Kālī!

It's the Kālī Yuga, not the happy butterfly Yuga. Grab your neighbors and huddle up for a few thousand years and pray like I taught you until this storm passes! Love one another as I have loved you. And when you can't, just keep f%#%ing trying, help is on the way.

For decades now, I've been deeply immersed in the world of Tantra and *the Divine Feminine*, and I wouldn't have it any other way. This path has been my refuge, my passion and above all else, the fire kund of transformation. Again and again, I have witnessed the profound awakening these ancient practices ignite: a luminous power that dissolves illusion and restores wholeness from the inside out.

In particular, the Mahavidyas, the Ten Wisdom Goddesses, have revealed themselves as profound allies for these times. Their presence is more than symbolic; it is catalytic. Each one a facet of the Great Goddess/Reality, they illuminate the hidden chambers of consciousness, pulling back the veil on who we *think* we are and revealing something far more beautiful (and sometimes slightly terrifying).

The Goddesses are not relics of a distant past, they're more like cosmic wake-up calls with impeccable timing. In a world that's overdosed on disconnection and rife with confusion, their message is refreshingly direct; no language or room for interpretation when your heart is on fire.

Despite all that I had learned, witnessed and experienced, this past year has been a year of discovery for me. For reasons I cannot fully explain or understand, most of my work has been with men, most of whom had never even heard of Tantra, let alone the Mahavidyas. Many of them are business leaders, professionals, fathers, husbands; busy people with full lives and packed calendars. Most had never before meditated. And not a single one could sit in any of the lotus postures.

Yet, something remarkable has been happening.

One after another, these men have begun to awaken and in the process, are rewriting the conventional wisdom around Kuṇḍalinī awakenings.

I share in more detail the awakening of one of the men in particular, who has also become a dear friend.

First of all, he's not at all comfortable in a yoga studio; or sitting on a meditation cushion for hours on end. He prefers pickup trucks, baseball caps and hanging out with his buddies. His language is more colorful than reverential. He is strong and carries a lived-in humility that only comes from having experienced life fully, as a father, husband, business leader. His wisdom isn't polished. It's raw, unvarnished and… *enthusiastic* (usually carrying an expletive, sometimes two).

He also, in his own words, *cries funny*, so he tries not to cry in public, yet can't stop sobbing whenever he speaks of God, or Grace as he calls it. He looks down at the ground when he weeps, and in those moments, his whole body shakes uncontrollably.

It has been a privilege to witness and guide his journey so intimately. He brought intensity, commitment and a willingness to learn. I fed him mantras and yogic disciplines, stories and scripture. He devoured it all.

What unfolded in him was unlike so many of *kuṇḍalinī* rising experiences I had seen. Very few dramatic *kriyās* or drama of any kind really. He made it his mission, at least at first, to resist the Goddess and her heart-melting bliss. I had never met anyone opposed to experiencing bliss but he seemed particularly focused and driven by something else entirely.

And while his effort to *resist the bliss* may well have been valiant at some level, it was also, well… absurd, and absolutely doomed to fail.

Not long after giving him his first mantra, he began experiencing 'odd' moments and would message me.

Sundari, I lost my truck today. Not as in I forgot where I parked, I mean I forgot what a truck even was. Is that normal? It all came back after a while but for about an hour I just sat in a coffee shop smiling for no reason and with no coffee.

I recommended, of course, a recipe for Ojas milk and a few herbal supplements to support and smoothen the unfolding. He instead opted to double down on his weightlifting regimen and increase his protein intake.

Yet, the unfolding was unstoppable. Some days, he couldn't help himself but stop beside random wildflowers just to take a photo.

And he made new friends. I remember one morning, sitting at a picnic table with him over coffee, when a stray cat leapt onto the table, just to lie down and rest her head on his outstretched arm. He didn't move his arm in the slightest, for fear of disturbing her peace.

I smiled and asked: *Do you like cats?*

He returned my smile and said flatly, *I don't.*

And occasionally, in moments of unbearable tenderness, he'd simply melt into a puddle of tears. The love he felt was so vast and uncontainable that his whole body shook. This he did publicly, more than once at my weekend immersions.

It was a glorious defeat; he went out on his shield, as the saying goes. I admired him for trying, truly. But let's be honest here: my dear friend was attempting to resist the *power of the Goddesses*. What exactly did he think was going to happen!?

To be clear, this man simply wasn't interested in blissful experiences.

Sundari, I don't want to disrespect any of the great work happening in

Tantra but I'm not here to get high or feel good, I'm here to become more skillful. I don't know if you've seen the news lately but the world I understand isn't exactly inspiring people with its nobility and wisdom. Feels like there is work to be done and if Tantra can help people find that taproot of clarity, courage and goodness, then we need a lot more of it and I want to help you any way I can.

He wasn't chasing ecstasy or transcendence. What he longed for was to bring the heavens down; to bring a little more light into his corner of the world. And the divine powers were indeed brought down, through tantric work, the power of mantra and the intensity of devotion. They found in him a strong vessel, ready to receive their blessings and offer them right back... through service to his fellows.

The ecstasy and transcendence just came for free, as part of that package.

As more men like my friend joined this year, a pattern began to emerge. The focus was rarely on attaining a particular state of consciousness. Instead, they seemed to approach the practice as a new kind of gladiatorial training: strength and conditioning for the heart and soul, alongside a refinement and sharpening of the mind.

This is in no way shared to diminish the women who have joined this past year; or those who have been walking this path with me for years. I could just as easily paint a remarkable picture of so many of the countless transformative journeys I have witnessed among the women.

And the freshness of what I experienced hasn't been only about men, whether they arrived in pickup trucks or otherwise, encountering the awakening power of Tantra. It's something deeper, more universal, that's been revealing itself through all who are ready.

What has been truly remarkable has been to witness firsthand the weaving and the fusion of forces that Tantra has long been known for. This alchemy between the Divine Masculine and Divine Feminine seems to amplify, accelerate and empower the work in profound ways. Even those who have been immersed in this path for years, well-acquainted with the energetic field that arises in Tantric immersions, have noticed a dramatic shift, both in terms of qualities and power.

What's also becoming more clear is this: on the journey of liberation and Self-Realization, there is strength in numbers, especially when those numbers include both men and women, striving side by side.

And perhaps most importantly, this work is becoming more accessible. Tantra has long been considered one of the more *esoteric* paths of awakening; but really, this just means its knowledge and practices haven't yet become widespread. Now, however, for people like my friend, who, in a topsy-turvy world, simply want to leave their corner of the world a little better than they found it, Tantra is offering a fast track to awakening, and a real way to do exactly that.

In the words of the illustrious sage Sri Ramana Maharshi, someone who indeed inspires with his nobility and wisdom:

Your own Self-Realization is the greatest service you can render the world.

Or in the words of my newly awakened friend:

Everyone is pretty much f*cked right now and that's ok. Better than ok actually because there is tremendous peace and great power in simply recognizing that. As an individual and as a society we are all somewhere between a little and a lot f*cked with no viable, rational path to get back to sanity, short of some great calamity.

It's nobody's fault and there are no villains to be found here, it's just the way things are. Once you really grok that reality and fall to your knees, surrendering to it with as much grace and acceptance as you can muster, something special will happen. Because right there, at the place where your knees touch the ground, is a wellspring of love and compassion that will never run dry. And from that place, amazing things will start to happen, for you and everyone around you.

And you will realize that this time, this exact era we are in right now, is one of great awakening. For thousands of years it's been said that one awakened person is like the rarest of miracles. Now just imagine, truly get your head and heart around this, the floodgates opening and this awakening happening by the tens of thousands every year. It's going to be amazing!

This to me feels, now, like the divine feminine version of an apocalypse. Not some great fire or torrential flood but regular folks just falling in love with each other, all around the world. Army generals and hedge fund managers running outside to snap a photo of a bird for reasons they can't explain or understand. Truly, it's going to be amazing!

Selected Essays & Reflections

GODS

&

GODDESSES

This is Tantra

Rumi was a Savage; or She is Black

·

Radical Love and the Kālī Devotee

"Every spiritual path hints at a distinct flavor of the kind of transformation that might follow. Some of the Buddhist paths for example suggest a profound level of equanimity and tranquility. A woman holding a severed head and a scimitar on the other hand hints at something different, and for me the path of Kālī is the path of radical love."

The form of the Goddess Kālī can be utterly bewildering especially for those who have been raised in a Western society where certain unconventional qualities and attributes of the feminine have been suppressed, distorted and tamed for the past few thousand years.

In this article I explore Kālī from both a classical tantric perspective as well as through the writings of one of my students who had a remarkable Kālī sādhana this year.

HAIR ON FIRE

A man wrote to me last year asking for guidance. He had been involved in spiritual practice for many years and made a point of daily journaling. One day he wrote something that puzzled him.

Sundari, you have to understand, for years my journals were the most banal grocery-list-type diary entries you could imagine. Real suburban hockey dad stuff and suddenly out pops this piece that is nothing like the others. I don't even know what I'm asking for here, but can you share more about Kālī? I feel some kind of affinity there but I don't have words to put around it.

After reading his 'puzzling' journal entry, we began speaking and this is where the intensity of his longing became clear. I was reminded of Ramakrishna Paramahansa, the well-known Hindu mystic and ardent devotee of Goddess Kālī, who was ready to take his own life if she did not reveal herself to him. This man carried that same fire.

Do not seek illumination unless you seek it as a man whose hair is on fire seeks a pond. - Shri Ramakrishna

While it's often said that, on the tantric path, we choose our ishṭa-devatā, the personal form of the divine that calls to us, here the teacher can help.

Ideally, the one who plays the role of the teacher, even if only temporarily, has the insight to recognize the divine powers at work within the student's psyche and consciousness. Such a teacher can nurture and support the student's deepening connection with the divine. In Tantra, the very act of transmitting spiritual power serves this purpose. It initiates the awakening process, bringing to light the divine power that was always hidden, just waiting to re-emerge.

The man eventually became my student. I initiated him into a Kālī sādhana and gave him a special mantra I had practiced for years. What unfolded from this point was remarkable. And though he asked to remain anonymous he agreed that I could share some of his writing in this article.

This is the journal entry that kick-started his process.

This thing we do, this game we play; deep inside your dark, past the shroud of your mystery I hear echoes of your laughter and I feel the lingering radiance of your smile, I'm getting closer.

Your longing betrays you now my dear that I am so near.

Which part did you love most this time? Was it your hiding or my seeking? Did you weep joyfully at my births or mourn sorrowfully at my deaths? Did you laugh rueful at my stubbornness, my slumbering mind and sleeping heart? Were you giddy with excitement at this little game of ours?

And in this our final chapter, did you shudder when I fell from grace? Did you clap when I rose triumphant, redeemed, awakened to your seduction?

Colder, colder. Warmer, warmer.

My heart evokes the faintest of memories; the delirious folly of it all, plunging into the amnesia and agony of Time; over and over, losing you for a thousand lifetimes. Millennia of suffering for one sweet singular moment. This one here now. That blissful hour that has most assuredly come. Our reckoning and reconciliation; the game has been won and the end draws near; you will be in my arms again.

Watch the lone Cossack on his horse, galloping the grassy steppe, devouring the ground with fierceness and indomitable will.

Almost. I am almost with you now.

KĀLĪ, SHAKTI AND TANTRA

In Tantra, life is celebrated and revered as the manifestation of the divine feminine power. This energy is known as Shakti, the Goddess, the eternal Beloved of Shiva. Shiva, the ultimate Silence of pure awareness, delights in resting in his cosmic hammock, while Shakti, the ever-creative Power, dances and plays to captivate him.

Though always One, Devī—*the Shining One*—expresses herself through her manifold faces, appearances and moods; some terrifying, some benevolent; some wild, others tender. Tantric sages have developed an intricate science to transform and elevate human consciousness by personifying these divine powers, engaging with them as the dazzling array of goddesses in the Hindu pantheon.

The Sanskrit word Kālī is the feminine form of Kāla, meaning time. She represents the supreme power that governs the universe. At its essence, time is eternal—everything changes, but change itself. Time is also relentless, devouring each moment and every experience, leaving us with nothing to cling to. Kālī and her wild sisters are among the most fearsome forms of the divine feminine, embodying the forces of transformation and, ultimately, liberation. To speak of yoga and inner alchemy without invoking Kālī would be like describing the sun without its blinding light.

In the *Bhairava Yāmala*, "She is Light itself and transcendent. Emanating from Her body are rays in thousands—two thousand, a hundred thousand, tens of millions, a hundred million—there's no counting their numbers. It is by and through Her that all things moving and motionless shine. It is by the light of this Devi that all things become manifest."

Known as the Supreme Reality in the non-dual tradition of Kashmir Shaivism, the Shakti is *vimarsha*—the free, luminous energy of self-awareness, manifesting itself successively in the form of twelve Kālīs or "the worlds from her womb". Ultimately, the Goddess is all there is. She's the fullness of consciousness. She is one with Shiva. They can never not be two, like the fire and its ability to burn. Shiva is Shakti in motion. The Primordial Power is ever at play as the power to be eternally conscious, the power to be unconditionally blissful, the power of unimpeded will, the power of intuitive knowledge and the power to act.

The Shakta doctrine places the *Dasha Mahāvidyās*, the shakti-cluster of the ten Great Wisdom Goddesses, each of them an embodiment of Kālī, is at the very heart of the teaching. The form of Kālī worshipped in Bengal is that of Mahāvidyā Kālī, according to Mookerjee in *Kālī: The Feminine Force*. Here, 'She, who is black' is welcomed into the homes as Divine Mother. In Kashmir, the goddess is venerated as Tripura Sundarī, the beauty of the three worlds, hinting at her all-encompassing power.

Kālī is the cosmic life-force, *prāṇa*, the tremor at the heart of existence. She is the electromagnetism between atoms and molecules, the polarity of attraction and repulsion, the womb of all creation. She is the raw force in a tiger's roar, the ground-shattering power of an earthquake, the magnetic red of a hibiscus flower, and the passion burning in a woman's heart.

In Kālī's name, where is there place for sin?

– Rāmprasād, Hindu Shakta poet and saint of 18th-century Bengal

In many traditions, the force of Kālī is revered as the Dark Mother, the fertility of the soil, the void, and the womb of new life. She is the power of sacrifice, birth and death, the cycle of existence itself. The ruler of time and the timeless, she cradles planets and galaxies as mere dust at her feet.

In her book Awakening *Shakti: The Transformative Powers of the Goddesses*, Sally Kempton describes a richly detailed traditional Nepali artwork in her home which showed Kālī in all her complex and significant symbolism.

The goddess is depicted as a strikingly beautiful young woman with dark blue skin, naked except for what looked like a "hula skirt" made of severed arms. Her round breasts were full and firm enough to burst off the canvas. Wild black hair flowed freely down her back and over her shoulders. Her wide, lustrous, sparkling eyes were set in a face so luminously beautiful that it was impossible not to be drawn to it. Her tongue stuck out just a bit, delicately touching her upper lip, and if you looked closely, a faint suggestion of fangs. In one of her four hands, a blood-dripping sword; in another, a freshly severed head. A necklace of skulls hung heavily as she squatted over the reclining form of Shiva, taking from him what she needed. Flames, blown by an invisible wind, flowed from Kālī's head and shoulders, and from Shiva's feet. One of her hands was raised in a mudra, signaling, "Fear not." Another of her hands pointed downward, bestowing boons.

Sally shared that visitors coming to her house would often sneak side glances at this image or stand in front of it for a few minutes, staring. She would humbly add that although she could rattle off the esoteric meaning of all those skulls and severed arms, this image reminded her simply that Kālī, as the fiercest aspect of the feminine, was not a goddess to take lightly.

THE POWER OF MANTRA SĀDHANA

Only weeks after he started the Kālī mantra *sādhana*, my student had begun sharing more of his writing with me. The process of transformation had begun, *this was abundantly clear*. The sheer volume of writing that flowed from him was staggering. Almost daily and sometimes multiple times on the same day I would receive notes from him. As an example, the note below was written spontaneously behind the wheel of his car, while sitting under a red traffic light.

Rumi was a savage. I need to atone for his sins.

To have slashed at your softness with desecrated husks and buried your splendor under graven images.

Forgive this man today my dear, he was heady and unsteady, legs weakened by your power and mind fogged by your fragrance. Forgive this barbarian that could not honor your grace with his silence. This man who stole a kiss and dared to speak, this drunken fool should be relieved from your grip that he may rest and sleep.

He was in the throes of the Kālī *sādhana*. The student, the mantra, the *sādhana* and the Goddess had in a sense all merged into what I could only then call a storm of grace that lasted months.

Initiation into a specific mantra *sādhana* is one of the tools on the spiritual path. The mantra works by transforming the samskaric field of the mind, the impressions, psychological tendencies and patterns that cloud our perception. As a sound vibration, the mantra reshapes how we see ourselves and the world. After all, everything we know about ourselves exists as thought constructs, essentially, sound.

Transformation begins at this very level. Dense, heavy vibrations are refined into the subtlest frequencies of consciousness, and the forms of these refined vibrations are the goddesses themselves. They are sound in embodied form.

When we chant a mantra, we invoke the goddess's form in our mind. There is a saying: *"You become what you behold,"* and this is precisely what unfolds. The divine, in the specific form invoked by the mantra, begins to take root within us, like a tiny seed sprouting and growing into a towering sequoia. Over time, we start to embody the divine power that is the essence of the sound vibration. In doing so, the grip of the person we thought we were loosens, as old patterns and synapses in our brain are quite literally rewired.

Sanskrit is a fascinating language, unique in that it remains the only vibratory language where form (*rupa*) and sound (*nama*) are still inseparably linked. This connection, broken in most other languages, means that the words we speak in Sanskrit directly invoke the essence of their meaning on a vibrational level. For instance, there is a specific sound for fire, and chanting it invokes the very quality of fire itself. In fact, there are yogis who, having mastered the power of mantra and their own minds, can ignite a spark of fire simply by uttering the word with one-pointed attention.

The opening mantra for this article is the supreme sound Om, called *pranava* or the original vibration. It is the unmanifest field behind creation from which all beings are born and into which all beings return.

The mantras to invoke Kālī embody the vibrational qualities of *prāṇa* (life force) and *agni* (fire). Her mantras are swift, fiery, sharp, and cutting. They generate transformative heat, burn away negativity, and offer protection—just as fire does. Each of the Shaktis has her own range of mantras, tailored to her essence and power. In the tantric tradition, it is understood that for a mantra to truly work, it must carry the consciousness of the teacher who has "cooked" it within the depths of their own heart. Only then does the mantra become a transmission; a key to unlock doors, a blessing that enables us to progress safely and swiftly on the path.

Kālī's mantras can be categorized into gentler *nama*(name) mantras and potent *bija* (seed) mantras. Some of her seed mantras are sharp, unpredictable and electrifying like lightning (*vidyut-shakti*) or a finely honed blade, and should only be practiced with clear understanding and intention. They are tools of immense power and, as such, should be invoked under the guidance of a teacher who knows their potency from firsthand experience.

RADICAL LOVE AND THE DARK MOTHER

Every spiritual path hints at a distinct flavor of the kind of transformation that might follow. Some of the Buddhist paths for example suggest a profound level of equanimity and tranquility. A woman holding a severed head and a scimitar on the other hand hints at something different, and for me the path of Kālī is the path of radical love.

The kind of love that is free from all judgement and condition; the kind of love that would indeed give someone the strength to *love thy enemy or bless them that curse you.*

The path of Kālī provides us with a gateway to this kind of love. Because as Alan Watts describes in his talk *She is Black*, the depiction of Kālī confronts us, starkly demanding that we move beyond any kind of conditioning or form the divine might take. It is the ultimate surrender of any and all concepts, including the most cherished beliefs, surrendering even the concept of *good* and *love* itself.

She provides us with the ultimate leap of faith, the jump into the void, that beyond all form and concept, lies something worth dying for.

I followed up with my student recently and asked if he could send me a quote for this article.

About Kālī? Use the least amount of words, just find the right picture: if you start with the feminine form, think firm but supple, hinting of sweat and mystery; you want a vibe of awe and astonishment at this perfect blend of infinite love and forgiveness with caramel swirls of vengeance and cruelty.

Then look at that picture and imagine the power within the man that can bring a Goddess like that to her knees; a man that can tame and satiate her both. Think of the devotion, suffering and sacrifice a man like that would have had to make along the way to gain the virtue needed for the journey. Now imagine her delight in each of those sacrifices that brought him closer to her.

Sense into the vibration of that space between them as they move towards each other and that final moment.

Or just put up a picture of the Sgr*A, the black hole at the center of this Milky Way... look closely at the folding and enveloping between the darkness and the light... feel the vibrancy of all the life you have ever witnessed and know that is nourished and sustained by that embrace.

Understand that you are not looking at some cold cosmological force but something deeply intimate and personal. You could even say the deepest and most personal picture you have ever seen.

And then if you are able to take it all in, you'll see there's no such thing as radical love, there is only Love. In all moments and things... her... and him... losing themselves and finding each other all over again in every atom and in every star, every innocent newborn and the dying breath of every scoundrel.

Just love one another as I have loved you, he said. But of course he did, truly, what else is there to say?

This is Tantra

Lakshmi and the Utpatti of Soma

•

An Offering Worthy of a Lady

"Lakshmi is the embodiment of beauty in its most radiant form. She is rich crops and bountiful harvests, the fertility of the land, and the lushness of forests. She is magnetic allure, generosity, tenderness, grace and charm. She is the lotus flower and the rose, the nectar for the bees, and the intoxicating bliss of life. In a sense, Lakshmi represents everything that makes life worth celebrating."

Hey ChatGPT - can you write a concise single paragraph on why Lakshmi is worshiped?

[ChatGPT] Lakshmi, the Hindu goddess of wealth and prosperity, is worshiped for her blessings of material and spiritual abundance, good fortune, and ethical success. She symbolizes balance between material wealth and spiritual growth, promoting the responsible use of resources for personal and societal well-being. Worshipping Lakshmi, especially during festivals like Diwali, invites prosperity, removes obstacles, and nurtures hope, gratitude, and positive energy, while honoring the divine feminine power she embodies.

Sally Kempton once shared a tale about the Goddess Lakshmi. It went something like this:

Once upon a time, Lakshmi and her consort Vishnu were living in the city of Varanasi, manifesting as the deities of a grand temple Jaganatha. This wasn't just any temple, it was the pinnacle of wealth and prestige, where only the upper castes were welcome.

This however didn't stop the poor and so-called untouchables to worship Lakshmi, with hearts full of devotion.

Then came Diwali, Lakshmi's festival of lights. On that special day, Lakshmi left the temple and made her way through the streets, visiting the homes of untouchables. House after house, she brought food, money, and blessings; not just to those who worshiped her, but even to those who didn't.

When Vishnu found out about Lakshmi's escapades, he was furious. "How could you mingle with untouchables?" he demanded, forbidding her from visiting them again.

Lakshmi was typically soft-spoken and compliant, but this time? Oh, she was not having it. She stormed out of the Jaganatha temple and moved in with the very people Vishnu disapproved of, a community of sweepers.

The sweeper community, once struggling to get by, suddenly flourished. Food appeared out of nowhere, crops sprouted up around their homes, and people started to rebuild their tiny huts. Meanwhile, back at Vishnu's temple? Things were falling apart. The offerings dwindled, the trees outside withered and the once-thriving temple became lifeless.

Realizing his mistake, Vishnu swallowed his pride, forgot about his status and went to the sweepers' neighborhood to beg Lakshmi for forgiveness. He asked her to come back. She listened quietly and said: "I'll come back, when you promise never to restrict my grace-giving impulses again." Well, Vishnu wasn't about to argue with the goddess of wealth. He agreed, and Lakshmi returned, bringing beauty and joy back to their abode.

A simple story, shared by a teacher like Sally, is not meant to be consumed and digested in one sitting. Often, these teachings will reverberate over the course of one's life; the tale as a fine bottle of wine, refining and maturing with time.

This story means something radically different today than when I first heard it some fifteen years ago.

In the Hindu tradition, the energy that nurtures and sustains all of life is personified as Lakshmi. She is worshiped as one of the principle goddesses, with incredible power at her fingertips. Her name, meaning the *auspicious* one, reflects her essence: prosperity, nourishment, success, good fortune, harmony, health, devotion, gentleness, and fullness.

Lakshmi is the embodiment of beauty in its most radiant form.

She is rich crops and bountiful harvests, the fertility of the land, and the lushness of forests. She is magnetic allure, generosity, tenderness, grace and charm. She is the lotus flower and the rose, the nectar for the bees, and the intoxicating bliss of life. In a sense, Lakshmi represents everything that makes life worth celebrating.

One of the original names for Lakshmi in the Indian tradition is *Shri*, a term that predates Lakshmi. Shri means *splendor* in Sanskrit, the beautiful light of the moon. It signifies beauty, auspiciousness, and shimmering greatness. This word encompasses everything magnificent and gentle in life. In the past, businessmen and politicians in India would begin official letters by drawing Shri at the top of the page, inviting auspiciousness and success into their affairs.

At its deepest, the vision of Lakshmi includes a sweet mind, a peaceful inner state where intrusive chatter has been surrendered. In Sanskrit, this is *chitta prasadanam*, a mind aligned with divine intention and service.

When Lakshmi is not acknowledged, she silently withdraws. Her absence leaves our hearts and the earth desolate; misery and misfortune take hold. Unlike the Goddess Kālī, who might disrupt with ferocity, Lakshmi simply fades, leaving us with feelings of disconnection and meaninglessness. Without her, we're impoverished. The sacredness of life is lost and forgotten.

WELTSCHMERZ AND LAKSHMI'S WITHDRAWAL FROM THE MODERN WORLD

I come across many people today in spiritual communities with deep feelings of disconnection, confusion, anxiety and depression. If the *sweet mind* is indeed Lakshmi's signature, then *Weltschmerz* would best describe her absence; a weary sense of world-pain that the realities of this will never fully satisfy and can only be escaped.

The past few decades have been marked by remarkable technological transformation. We are living through a period of acceleration where the amount of change in any given decade is likely more than what past generations experienced in an entire lifetime.

Whatever achievements this civilizational period may claim, they have come at a cost. For many, the basic nourishing bonds of family, community and ancestry have been all but sacrificed. It's no wonder, so many people feel disconnected because so many are actually disconnected; and it's no surprise that so many people feel a sense of world-pain, because indeed, the world is in pain. Lakshmi has withdrawn from the temple.

We are living through a period of deep, root-and-branch-level-transformation and of today's modern spiritual practitioners, more is being asked. The ChatGPT version of Lakshmi sādhana: placing a few laddhus on a shrine and 108 Lakshmi japa mantras, will not be enough to overcome the push and pull of the times.

AWAKENING AS DUTY AND AN OFFERING WORTHY OF A GODDESS

It is a widely held belief that the spiritual journey is a solitary affair. That somehow, the path to self-realization or enlightenment must be undertaken solely through one's own initiative and for one's own sake. Even some great masters have lamented the occasional bouts of loneliness that accompany this journey. And the conventional belief is that a householder must sacrifice their responsibilities to fully devote themselves to *awakening*.

Consider this however, whatever spiritual path a person can take today, it is only possible because of thousands of people doing their jobs.

Ingredients for Ayurvedic soup and supplements are delivered on time; internet connections for online darshans are maintained and aircraft piloted by professionals get used to undertake pilgrimages. *No person is an island*, as the saying goes, has never been more true than in this era of interconnectedness.

Recently, I've begun asking my students during meditation immersions: *Who are you undertaking this spiritual work for? What ideals are you sacrificing yourself for? You meditate and seek awakening so that... what? Put differently, who or what in your life is worth dying for?*

While this might seem dramatic, consider that our societies still ask every young soldier to answer this question.

The opportunity here lies in an important reframing of spiritual practice. For anyone seeking the profound awakening of the tantric path, the journey must be seen as one of service to something greater. Awakening as a sacrifice: a sacred, noble duty offered on behalf of one's family, community, nation; or even this very same soldier standing lonely, guarding the temple gates.

We meditate, pray, gather, and serve as a form of offering that the nourishing power of Lakshmi and the heavens can flow back into our communities. The sādhana here, being performed with the intensity and commitment of a devotional heart.

The possibility is given for the student to offer themselves fully not for personal gain, but in service of the greater whole. It is the deepest dive into the soul's depths so that more light can enter the world and all arenas of life.

It is asking absolutely nothing of Lakshmi and offering absolutely everything.

All that you are and all that you will ever be, offered at the feet of such a Goddess with the faintest of hopes that her restorative touch can be felt by a world desperately missing her nurturing. *So that through* your sacrifice and devotion, this world is one person closer to the magnetic allure, generosity, tenderness, grace and charm Lakshmi is celebrated for.

This is not ChatGPT yoga, this is the all-in-tantric-sacrifice where the student will not even live out to see the fruits of his or her own service. It is Love sacrificing itself to Love for the sake of Love. *So that through* your hands Lakshmi can do her work and through your eyes she can smile upon the earth.

The entire inner science of yoga is rooted in the understanding of the power of sacrifice, *yajna* in Sanskrit, translated: *Worshiping the Supreme Lord or Rendering service to the Supreme Lord.*

THE UTPATTI OF SOMA

In writing this piece, it was very easy for me to find the most appropriate word in *Weltschmerz* that I needed to capture this feeling of world-pain. But in searching for another very specific word for a subtle feeling, I couldn't find what I was looking for; either in German or English.

The closest I could come is in Sanskrit and that word is *utpatti*.

The feeling here is one of a certain kind of *arising*. It is the impulse in all things to sweeten and nourish. It is the moment the flower decides to produce nectar or the impulse of the maple to produce its sweet sap. It is this arising Lakshmi impulse that drove Babylon to build the Hanging Gardens and the same utpatti that randomly makes us want to call an old friend and nurture the relationship.

For me, this is what the path of Tantra is essentially concerned with: working with others to facilitate the *utpatti* of Soma; the blissful restoration of the sacred and the numinous within a person's life, extending to their relationships, family and community. And maybe even to this age we live in as a whole.

While this technological era has certainly come at a cost, it has also provided incredible opportunity. The speed and scale with which we can communicate today is certainly a wonder in its own right.

Thanks to the interconnectedness of today, this utpatti of soma in the life of a single person can have a radical ripple effect on hundreds, maybe even thousands, or more. The sweet mind of one awakened being can spontaneously ignite the sweet mind in another, and so on. It's not impossible to imagine the return of civilizational wonders, like the Hanging Gardens, in less than a generation.

The return of Lakshmi to her temple, and the sweetening, nourishing impulse at the core of our societies may not be as far away as what one might think. The wholehearted sacrifice of a few today will have a profound effect on the many tomorrow.

Jai Sita Ram and The Snake Who Ate Its Own Tail

•

A peek inside my heart

"That somehow the evolution of the human soul is so profoundly valued and we are but brave children serving in the vanguard at the forefront of this progression. That the price of evolution is our shared suffering; and when our suffering gets too much, in our darkest and most agonizing moments, our cries will never be in vain. The hero of the Gospels, the Tender One, will forever be there for us."

This is Tantra

This essay began as an attempt to capture the divine romance portrayed in the epic Ramayana. I wanted to explore the subtle interplay between the divine feminine and masculine in the characters of Sita and Ram.

Instead, I was swept away, yet again, by my love of Hanuman, the heroic monkey who (spoiler alert) vanquishes the demons and rescues the princess. Beautiful Hanuman who in the end, defers all glory and declines all reward, asking instead simply to be of eternal service.

The writing is now less of an essay and more of an offering. To Hanuman, Jesus of the Gospels and the love story at the heart of human evolution; it is a peek inside my own heart.

The good news for today's spiritual aspirants is that we are living in an unprecedented time. Never before in recorded history have so many lineages, teachings and practices been so easily accessible, just a phone swipe away.

This, unfortunately, is also the bad news. The modern spiritual landscape has become a dense jungle. Buried treasures to be sure but also hungry predators.

This is especially true when stepping into more esoteric and powerful traditions like Tantra where the impact and effects of practice can be rapid and deeply transformative. Over the years I've witnessed sincere practitioners stumble or get lost on this path, often painfully, simply because they were lacking the ground to stand on or were not sure what this was all about.

If I could offer just a single recommendation to those walking this path, it would be this: keep the classics close at hand. Turn to the timeless stories and scriptures that have passed through the hands and hearts of countless generations. Works like the *Bhagavad Gita*, the *Yoga Sutra of Patanjali* or the *Tao Te Ching* have served as steady companions on my journey, anchor points I've returned to again and again when the path grew dense or unclear.

And of course, the *Ramayana*. A spiritual epic packed into a mythic fairy tale of sorts.

At its core, the *Ramayana* is something of a cosmic romcom: boy meets girl, boy loses girl, boy enlists a magical monkey to help save the day. But this isn't just any boy - it's Ram, the princely incarnation of Vishnu, the sustaining power of the cosmos. And the girl is Sita, none other than Goddess Lakshmi, Vishnu's eternal consort.

Sita is captured and enslaved by the antagonist of the story, the ten-headed demon king, Ravana. But here's a slight twist, Ravana isn't just your typical villain. He's a devoted spiritual practitioner himself, a master of the Vedas and a formidable warrior. And yet... he somehow still ends up with nine extra heads and an immense appetite for kidnapping women.

Ravana perhaps here, serves as a potent warning to aspirants that even spiritual masters may not always embody the kind of virtues the spiritual path implies.

Enter Hanuman. A monkey-god, born of a virgin. His mother, once a celestial being, had been cursed to live life on Earth in the form of a monkey-like creature. Yet she never forgot her origin and through her intense devotion, the heavens responded. A divine wind swept through her, and she conceived a son. Hanuman was born, part monkey, part god.

As a young monkey, Hanuman had no idea of the power within him. Always curious and ever ready for mischief, he mistook the sun for a ripe mango hanging in the sky. Leaping upwards, Hanuman ate the sun, plunging the world into darkness. The gods were not amused. They cursed him with forgetfulness, so he would not remember his powers unless and until someone reminded him. And so Hanuman grew up entirely unaware of what was hidden within.

It was on meeting Ram for the first time and hearing of Ram's love for Sita that something ancient awakened within him. He was inspired by the depth of Ram's love, and in turn, Ram was moved by Hanuman's humility. An eternal bond was formed, and the rest of the epic flows from here.

I choose to interpret this moment between Ram and Hanuman today as a threshold-moment on the path, the moment of awakening. Call it self-realization, illumination, recognition, or whatever conceptual language seems adequate to mark this turning point in our evolution.

Something essential is revealed in that moment, and from it, a new kind of power begins to flow into a person's life. History is filled with such moments, etched into the lives of great saints, sages and mystics across the ages.

What sets the *Ramayana* apart, however, is how Hanuman distinguishes himself from Ravana. Where Ravana seeks ever-increasing power to cement his own plans and ambitions, Hanuman rejects it all. He asks for nothing, desires nothing for himself, and offers himself fully at the feet of Ram.

> **Deha buddhi se dasa,**
> **Jiva buddhi se tuma sakha,**
> **Atma buddhi se tuma mama.**
>
> *As long as I identify with the body, I am your servant;*
> *when I identify with the soul, I am your friend;*
> *and when I realize the Self, I am one with you.*

This dialogue, later refined:

> **When I do not know who I am, I serve You.**
> **When I know who I am, I am You.**

The devotion expressed in these lines is particularly worthy of contemplation for students on non-dual (*advaita*) paths. Many advaita teachers focus only on oneness and forget the devotion (*bhakti*) entirely. I have witnessed firsthand the damage that this approach can cause.

Closer to home, this would be like Jesus entering the Judean desert for 40 days, realizing the Self and then walking off to live out his days in a remote cave. By moment blissful and ecstatic. The end.

Somehow this story doesn't carry the same power.

And speaking of classics, The Gospels; or as C.S. Lewis elucidates in this talk, *what are we to make of Jesus Christ?*

Like the *Ramayana*, the Gospels serve as rich food for contemplation; and likely will reveal deeper layers of meaning over the course of one's spiritual unfolding.

For me, as a young woman growing up in a contemporary, liberal German household, the Gospels took on the air of the folklore of a quaint but bygone era.

Later, as I made the rounds of Indian ashrams and temples, diving deep into Hindu and tantric scripture and practice, it was challenging to reconcile the Jesus of the Gospels with the teachings I was receiving. The two seemed worlds apart.

Jesus did not speak in terms of enlightenment like the Buddhists, or self-realization like Krishna in the Gita. Jesus, at least at first glance, did not offer mantra or breathing practices like the *Shiva Sutras*, the *Vijnana Bhairava Tantra* or the *Hatha Yoga Pradipika*.

Yet many great Hindu sages have spoken of Jesus, sometimes even laying claims that during the missing pages of his youth, he visited a particular temple or practiced his sādhana with this or that well-known lineage.

For legendary yogis like Ramakrishna Paramahansa, Sivananda Saraswati and Paramahansa Yogananda, the figure of Christ loomed large. And in a world of legendary gurus and realized beings, Jesus remains a perplexing figure.

He overcame the world, and then, defiantly, dove right back into it. Why?

For any spiritual student this is so deeply worthy of meditation and contemplation. To feel into the heart-qualities of a man walking slow but steadfast back towards civilization after 40 days in the desert. Not an ounce of fat on his body, his clothes ragged and dirty, his skin blistered but then to imagine his eyes radiating the fire of determination. Having conquered every demon and passed every test. Walking stoically, knowing exactly what lay ahead and what had to be done.

In contemplating the Gospels, some parallels with the *Ramayana* can be drawn. The epic nature of the unfolding of events for example. Or the heroic virtues shared by both Hanuman and Jesus. But this is where the similarities end because what is most striking for me today: the Gospels feel like a complete inversion of the *Ramayana*.

The Indian epic is aristocratic, featuring Gods, princes, princesses and lords. The Gospels touch on fallen women, lepers and tax collectors.

The *Ramayana* is regarded as a masterpiece of prose, filled with breathtaking scenes, vivid metaphors and dialogue. The Gospels, by contrast, read more like an excited child recounting to his mother the story of something incredible that happened on his first day of school.

Hanuman's example of heroic devotion towards God, inverted to

Jesus' heroic devotion towards humanity:

'These things I have spoken unto you, that in me ye might have peace. In the world ye shall have tribulation: but be of good cheer; I have overcome the world.'

Spoken right before his arrest and crucifixion.

Finally, the iconography of Hanuman opening his heart, and revealing Sita and Ram glowing luminously inside, is painfully turned around with the agony of a dying Christ and the sounds of a wailing mother.

Hanuman's love of God, in the life of Jesus is reversed into God's love of *us*.

You and me, glowing luminously, cherished and held so tenderly inside the Great Heart.

That somehow the evolution of the human soul is so profoundly valued and we are but brave children serving in the vanguard at the forefront of this progression. That the price of evolution is our shared suffering; and when our suffering gets too much, in our darkest and most agonizing moments, our cries will never be in vain. The hero of the Gospels, the Tender One, will forever be there for us.

'Come to me, all who labor and are heavy laden, and I will give you rest. Take my yoke upon you, and learn from me, for I am gentle and lowly in heart, and you will find rest for your souls. For my yoke is easy, and my burden is light.'

If the *Ramayana* is a story about humanity's love of the Divine, then today for me, the Gospels reflect God's love of humanity. They are a message from on high, proclaimed for all people during a dark and difficult time:

In your stumbling you are seen, and in your striving you are loved.

This is Good News indeed. Terrific news even!

Jai Sita Ram!

-Sundari Ma

Laying Down Arms: Chhinnamasta and the Battle of the Sexes
•

Everything is an Image of the Ecstasy of the Creator

"You, me, us, are the rarest of cosmic miracles. And we struggle and we fight, buffeted by ignoble winds we can never hope to understand, striving for a love we will never fully grasp. We were the glint in Eve's eye and our very own life is what Shiva sacrificed himself for."

Eve! Don't... wait... don't eat the apple! He exclaimed.

Once they were two, happy as only young lovers could be. Alone together in paradise. But it wasn't quite enough. She wanted a little bit more.

It was the snake! She said coyly with a glint of mischief in her eye.

And thus the great debate of the ages began. Why oh why did Eve reach for that apple?

Like Adam and Eve of the Old Testament, Tantric tradition is rich with scripture, symbolism and great epics poetically capturing the interplay between the masculine and feminine.

In several past articles, I have written about the Dasha Mahavidyas. These ten wisdom goddesses are foundational to Tantric practice, each representing a specific aspect of the divine feminine power that governs and marshals the very forces of life. It is worth underlining here, however, that while the Mahavidyas often take center stage, they each operate in relation to Shiva, the power of the divine masculine, more rarely mentioned, yet ever-present.

Much like in the Genesis story, where it is Eve who brings dynamism and sets events in motion, the Mahavidyas represent the dynamic forces that move us and shape us against the backdrop of the silence of Shiva. This is perhaps best illustrated by the goddess Chhinnamasta, who was the central theme of my recent tantric meditation weekend.

For those readers who have never attended a practical tantric workshop, the term workshop is a bit of a misnomer. These weekends invite the unknown and carry intensity for everyone involved. Rather than instructional sessions, they are full tantric immersions, where students can access depth of experience and levels of transformative energy not otherwise encountered in regular practice.

On this particular weekend, I sat and held the space near the front in a cozy sunlit yoga room. Seated in a circle, ten students evenly split between men and women. Beside me, on a small wooden table, an altar had been arranged with a Shiva lingam facing a bronze statue of Chhinnamasta hidden beneath a drape of orange fabric.

The drape wasn't ceremonial as much as practical.

Chhinnamasta is the fiercest amongst the Dasha Mahavidyas, *Prachanda Chandika*, the blazing one. Kālī's wildest sister, or, Kālī's most radical form. Her iconography can be unsettling for most people.

She stands boldly, legs apart, atop a naked couple locked in a sexual embrace. In one hand, she holds her own freshly severed head. In the other, a scimitar. And from her headless neck, three streams of blood gushing like a living fountain: one flows into the mouth of her own severed head, the other two are drunk by her female attendants flanking her on either side.

Perhaps a little heavy for the first session on a Friday night. On Saturday morning however, the veil was lifted and the goddess greeted the group so-to-speak.

Students were invited to describe what they saw and share whatever was evoked. The reactions were divided more or less equally between muted and polite. As far as iconography goes, the Mahavidyas resist any kind of easy categorization or simplification the mind might attempt. But as the discussions progressed so did the tension build as is typical in these immersions when the fierce Mahavidyas are invoked.

Beneath the initial agreeable observations, the deeper emotional undercurrents began to stir. The obvious symbolism of Chhinnamasta is around sacrifice and conception which drew the discussion towards *parents*. One by one, the childhood wounds surfaced. Pain. Acrimony. Enmity and sadness. Carried silently through the adult years and buried beneath the success and glitter of a fast paced life. Subtly, the room started to take on the energy of a pediatric ward.

This is Tantra on weekend. Chhinnamasta and her fierce sisters, bringing all grievances and contrivances to the surface of our awareness. And in the safety and intimacy of this shared space, their presence is an invitation to lay down arms and be with what is.

Laying down arms... making peace is the first step towards any kind of meaningful and lasting spiritual progress, whatever the lineage or faith. While love thy enemy may well be a bridge too far for many to cross, an armistice with mom and dad or their memories is a big step forward in that journey.

This is not forgiveness or any concept of right and wrong at all really, it is simply taking a moment to just be with the truth of our own lives. And that's where the Shakti took us that weekend. The name of every father was spoken, and their stories were brought into the light. Smiles, lowered voices, tears, anguish and sometimes just silence. After that the names of the mothers, and stories with similar emotional outpourings.

The alchemy of the room had been transformed into one of great tenderness. Like all the fierce Dasha Mahavidyas, Chhinnamasta is a pathway to a deep and tranquil love; the heart quality that emerges after the storm has passed, exuding humility, gratitude and gentleness along with the maturity of understanding, that, yeah, life can be pretty rough at times; for all beings across all of time. *Welcome to the planet kids.*

The room was a tiny sample of the population at large. But it's clear that while, on one level, our societies appear terrifically successful and technologically brilliant, at the very core, we are a wounded people; children of the revolution, casualties of a war nobody remembers starting.

And the tantric approach here is not about healing wounds or correcting perceived sins of the past, but about making peace with *life as it is* for just long enough to glimpse a deeper truth. The one that suggests that maybe, just maybe, it's all perfect and so are we. And maybe Eve knew exactly what she was doing when she ate that apple.

In a sense, Chhinnamasta, offers us a divine feminine *Story of Job*, where in his despair and anguish a man questions the will of God. And God in the form of a whirlwind answers with a question of his own.

Who is this that darkens counsel by words without knowledge? Gird up your loins like a man; I will question you, and you shall declare to me. Where were you when I laid the foundation of the earth?

Followed by verse after verse of question from God to Job that emphasize the point, if you really want to find fault with those that gave you form and that which gives you breath, be prepared to stand your ground and take responsibility for the whole thing.

THE FATHER'S SACRIFICE.

Less prominent in the Chhinnamasta scene is the male figure at the base supporting the female figures above. Shiva here, stepping forward and lying down, not as conqueror, but as the sacrificial giver. Offering his seed, his light, his presence and most of all, eternal support and devotion, to her and all what will come from her.

The Great Sacrifice of the One into the many; he gives her all that he is and all he will ever be. I asked a student of mine, also a father, about this idea of a father's sacrifice and he smiled and said: *One of the men who survived the Titanic spent the rest of his life living in shame. Women and children first. It is like that. It might not be like that for all men, but I'd imagine it is like that for most.*

In my version of the cosmic love story, when One became Two, he thought two would be enough for eternity. Shiva holding Shakti in his eternal embrace, not for a second believing she could possibly want more. Whoops.

In this version, Chhinnamasta, represents the power of conception and all that is given into that moment. So much is given that one wonders why two lovers would ever dream of doing this in the first place. And here Tantra hints delicately at this, and perhaps even a clue as to why Eve ate the apple to set a great story in motion.

Because... well, because - *you*.

You dear reader. Out of this cosmic maelstrom you, me, us emerged. Each of us, a life so perfectly unique, destined never to be repeated exactly the same way. We are the finite, so preciously held within the love and light of the infinite.

You, me, us, are the rarest of cosmic miracles. And we struggle and we fight, buffeted by ignoble winds we can never hope to understand, striving for a love we will never fully grasp. *We* were the glint in Eve's eye and our very own life is what Shiva sacrificed himself for.

She saw in us life abundant in all its confused glory, the bitter and the sweet, the cruel and the nourishing and in Her infinite wisdom, knew the perfection of the entire unfolding. We are the vanguard of evolution, keeping a campfire going for the children of tomorrow.

This is what distinguishes Tantra from other great noble paths. It is less about peaking behind the curtains and attaining this or that state of consciousness and more about fully realizing the depth and wonder of our own life.

And the first step to living that wonder is to make peace with life as it is and letting go of any and all notion of the way it should be. To acknowledge and appreciate, if only for an interval, that somewhere along the way, a sacrifice was made for each of us to be here.

A few days after the weekend, one of the participants came to my regular lunchtime meditation session. There was something different about him that day, an unmistakable glow, as if a door to another world had been left slightly ajar within him. The glow and the easy smile, suggesting to me he had touched the wonder of his own being.

He meditated quietly and peacefully in a gentle midday sunlight filtered by the trees outside. And then he laid down to rest in a relaxed fetal position with his bare feet sticking out beyond the edge of his blanket. After he got up, he looked at me as if he wanted to share something.

And then he spoke:

It was a little strange Sundari. I heard a voice. It was so crisp and so powerful. And it asked me a simple question but in a forceful way that demanded a prompt answer. The question confounded me, maybe because I don't usually hear voices, but mostly because the answer was so obvious.

Who are you? Boomed the voice.

I am my Father's Light and my Mother's Love. I answered.

Who else could I possibly be?

This is Tantra

Acacia Trees and The Living Field of Bhuvaneshwari

Love on the Autobahn of Life

"Tantric legends abound with stories of this field's incredible power. Over the years, I'd had many glimpses of it; those moments when a room of people meditating settles, and you can almost hear the heartbeat of God pulsing in the silence. But the full miracle-like power of the enlivened field, the kind that ancient texts sometimes described as myth, had always seemed a bit like... well, myth.

Until this year."

Last Easter weekend marked the one year anniversary since stepping out as a tantric teacher. In this article, I reflect on the wonder of this year and on Bhuvaneshwari, one of the most elusive tantric Wisdom Goddesses, yet perhaps the most important for our time.

There's no general speed control on German highways; it's a paradise for speed demons and a mild nightmare for anyone just trying to visit their grandparents without needing therapy afterward. Not exactly a place to find love.

Yet, there was a loving moment I remember vividly from my childhood.

Somewhere up ahead there had been an accident and every driver on the autobahn began to behave in an unusual way, completely in harmony. The frantic speeders and the Sunday drivers in the right lane suddenly moved together, like a flock of birds turning midair or a school of fish sensing the shift of a hidden current. Lights flashed, hands waved, rescue lanes opened as if choreographed by some unseen intelligence. For a few timeless moments, it felt to me as if the whole world was wrapped in a soft, invisible presence.

At the time, this moment felt magical, miraculous even. Later, I learned that I had experienced what Tantra describes as *Goddess Bhuvaneshwari*, one of the *Dasha Mahavidyas* (ten wisdom goddesses) or aspects of the divine feminine that govern life and our evolution.

Bhuvaneshwari, the great Queen of Space, isn't just some abstract cosmic concept. She's the *field of existence* itself, the living spaciousness where everything dances into being. All places are her body; all beings move through her infinite heart. She is the ground beneath our feet, the breath in our lungs, the ecstatic yes behind creation itself.

And yet say the Tantrics: she's also a goddess with a very real personality. She lounges on a jeweled bed, with dark red eyes, delicate lips, and a beauty so overwhelming she cannot be fully contemplated. Breasts dusted with sandalwood and earrings sparkling in the form of the Shri Yantra. In one hand she holds a goad, because sometimes the world needs a nudge and in another, a bowl spilling over with jewels. Her other hands are in motion busy giving boons and blessings or waving away fear and anxiety. Fear not dear child, I am with you always.

But what truly makes her irresistible is her heart. This indeed can be contemplated and intimately felt.

Bhuvaneshwari is the cosmic master of love. Not the clingy, check-if-you-read-my-text-message kind of love. The real thing. She is *iccha-shakti*, the divine will that says, *slow down child, relax into your life, you belong here, take up some space and grow something beautiful.*

Her love doesn't hover nervously or panic if we miss a call. No. It's vast and calm, like a summer field stretching out under a sky big enough for every dream we've ever had. It gives us room to breathe, stumble and bloom in our own wildly imperfect way. When love doesn't offer that kind of space, it's the conditional kind of love, trying its best but clinging too tightly and accidentally suffocating the very thing it wants to admire.

Bhuvaneshwari's love, by contrast, unhooks the claws of fear. She teaches us that real love doesn't obsess over appearances or clutch at forms as they pass. True love celebrates the vastness itself, the spaciousness that holds all of it, birth and death, sorrow and song, side by side.

And it's through her kind of love that we're lifted beyond our personal agendas. We forget ourselves for a prolonged breath. And through that gap, grace sweeps in. Suddenly, strangers love each other for no good reason and a highway full of busy, separate lives becomes one living body, moving with a single heartbeat.

The following writing was shared with me by one of my dear students following his 40-day Bhuvaneshwari sādhana.

Dear Sundari,

I have completed the 40 day sādhana. Once again, I find myself surprised and delighted at the power of these mantras. I am however a little embarrassed to share that I still cannot pronounce her name with ease the way you do. I say it slowly in small words like a toddler, Bhu-va-ne-shwa-ri.

More importantly though, less than halfway through the sādhana I realized that I have encountered her before. Several times actually but two in particular stand out for me.

Once in the Masai Mara, the Kenyan side of the Serengeti. I was there during the Great Migration with zebras and wildebeest as far as the eye can see. Think Tokyo or New York City but on the plains and rolling hills of the savannah.

And they got those big acacias there. Flat top umbrellas with branches out of reach for even the tallest giraffes.

Bhuvaneshwari: I felt her before I saw her. That still small voice, guiding me, urging me gently to shift my gaze away from the herds toward the ungrazen still tall red oat grass. I watched a gentle breeze rustling through pointing to a lone acacia tree yonder. Not a creature to be seen there, just the flattening of the hills and the dry whisper of the oat stalks yet to be grazed. The gust dissipated into the shade of the acacia's umbrella while the tree stood sentinel under the cloudless sky, regal like, a great lord of some kind or other, pulling the heavens down and nourishing all of creation.

She stayed with me while I turned back to watch wildebeest forming a caravan that stretched back miles. They organized into the longest queue I had ever seen, nose to tail moving in unison towards a crossing point of a dried up riverbed out of reach of the crocodiles. Behind them zebras grazed the short grass in packs of threes. The guide said they did this to ward off the lion huntresses stalking in the taller grass not so far away. In the same sweep of landscape, off in the distance I could see an oxpecker riding the lonely bull elephant roaming the horizon. All under the auspices of that acacia. The moment was crystal clear, then and now, all creation is her dominion and I am by moment witness and servant both.

Bhuvaneshwari was also with me in the suburbs once. A fleeting encounter while sitting on a parking lot curb with my boy. Thirty minutes to kill waiting for my girls to finish their dance lesson on an otherwise busy Saturday. Absolutely nothing to do except share an orange juice and take in the crisp early spring air together.

The stillness of that moment pulled me in. And I watched my boy while a little something in me started to tingle. His little paw-like hands, trying to grip the orange juice bottle. His arms, not reliably able to bring it to his mouth. His head tilting way too far back and my daddy instinct kicking in that some gentle cleanup would be required. I watched as the sun slowed down to light his hair just so, shades of ochre and hues of red and orange I had never seen before. The birds above hung mid air while my heart swelled and tears streamed down my face.

Cormac McCarthy wrote - "If he isn't the word of God, then God never spoke". And it was like that for me at that moment. The recognition of the magnitude of this child's life and my role in it. Here he was, the word of God radiating his innocence totally unspoiled but for the juice trickling down his cheek. He belonged to her but he was my ward and I'd been entrusted with a sacred duty. That's Bhuvaneshwari: crystal clear clarity on a Saturday morning with parking lot pigeons flying overhead.

It happens like that sometimes. If Kālī is the Goddess who annihilates time, Bhu-va-ne-shwa-ri is who is left, cradling a boy in a bright yellow jacket and rosy cheeks with flecks of orange juice yet to be wiped. She is Eckart Tolle's Power of Now plus tears of awe and gratitude; She is at the intersection of me and here, heart agape, bursting with love and dutiful care for all creation.

I will never be able to thank you enough for re-introducing me to Bhuvaneshwari.

Yours

-AT

As Alex alludes to in his note, tantric sādhana doesn't just help us find inner peace, it reveals the power of the Goddess who is ever present. Suddenly, we recognize her with awe and a conscious connection to the Great Heart awakens. The *living field of grace* is enlivened by one more heart.

According to the ancient teachings, this field is an energetic matrix in which spontaneous healing and synchronicity arise. And more importantly, the sages knew that it's possible through joint practice to stir and excite this field, to increase its loving power and to expand its reach.

Tantric legends abound with stories of this field's incredible power. Over the years, I'd had many glimpses of it; those moments when a room of people meditating settles, and you can almost hear the heartbeat of God pulsing in the silence. But the full miracle-like power of the enlivened field, the kind that ancient texts sometimes described as myth, had always seemed a bit like... well, myth.

Until this year.

In our little desert yoga studio here in Dubai, something remarkable began to unfold: People who had never meditated before came walking into the gathering, sat down, and almost instantly dropped into transcendence, this jewel-like state of pure Being. They didn't know the terminology. They hadn't memorized any mantras. And yet, there they were, held in the golden silence.

Normally, and by that I mean, traditionally, these Samadhi states don't yield so much transformation. Until a consistent practice can be established that leads to a radical shift in perception, there's little integration of the inner union with the affairs of the world. The elevated experience is almost forgotten as soon as it takes place.

But to my astonishment, complete newcomers, never having meditated, showed up at the studio, took a few breaths, and disappeared into samadhi; then walking out transformed in unique ways. Awake. With shining eyes. Husbands and wives falling in love all over again. Familial bonds tightening, old acquaintances receiving surprise phone calls. Faces softening into radiant joy. Grievances and traumas dissolving like mist in the morning sun. Life, starting to reorganize itself in ever more beautiful and synchronistic ways, as Bhuvaneshwari's invisible hand seemed to effortlessly rearrange fate itself.

New meditation slots were scheduled - lunchtime sessions in the middle of a busy workday. People began dropping by, and week after week, the field grew stronger. Inner spaciousness and velvety peace became outer reality, boundaries between me and you began to shimmer and blur, until all that remained was the shared pulse of one Being, breathing through many faces.

The *One, Whose Body is the World* doesn't discriminate. She doesn't check our credentials at the door. All are her children. All are worthy of the highest. No organizations. No robes. Just one simple requirement: *You are human? Perfect. Welcome back into the arms of love. Feel better? Good. Now go home and be a little kinder.*

And in the fertility of such an excited field, something extraordinary is born. Not the puff-of-smoke-rabbit-in-the-hat-miracles but something far more remarkable: strangers starting to care about one another and the world. Genuine and attentive, effortless and without thought of praise or glory. Not through some urgent call to action, but because it is simply who we are. This is *us*, humans, in our most natural state.

The supreme, secret, miraculous power of Bhuvaneshwari's enlivened field... is to oh-so-graciously and oh-so-tenderly, lay us bare and strip away the bullshit and made up things for just long enough to experience *this* Reality, where we fall to our knees in joy and reverence at the miracle of it all.

Absent the world of abstract and made-up things, we take care of each other. We heal the sick, hold the grieving and share our good fortune with those less fortunate.

The arc of nature in harmony bends towards goodness. And so do we.

This is the great healing hand of the goddess that will weave its way through our time. The power of this field will only grow now. Bhuvaneshwari's love does not abate.

More people will come, drawn by the simple, irresistible call to *belong* to something timeless again. And here, in the shelter of a desert yoga studio, we will go on doing the simplest, most revolutionary thing possible: sitting gently and breathing into silence together on a lunch hour.

And I am so incredibly grateful to everyone who has joined me on this magical journey so far, and to all who have helped and supported me in so many ways behind the scenes this past year.

May this field blossom like a garden of wild flowers.

May it benefit all who come close.

May love reign supreme.

Om Hrīm Shrīm.

The mountain Arunachala (Holy Hill) in Tiruvannamalai, Tamil Nadu state, South India, is one of the oldest and most sacred holy places associated with Lord Shiva in India.

Red Hibiscus, the flower used for Kālī offerings.

One day the Goddess sang to her lover, Bhairava:

*"Beloved and radiant lord of the space before birth,
I have been listening to the hymns of creation,
Enchanted by the verses,
Yet still I am curious.*

*What is this delight-filled universe
Into which we find ourselves born?
What is this mysterious awareness
Shimmering everywhere within it?"*

Bhairava replies,

*"Beloved, your questions
Touch the heart of wonder,
The path of intimacy with all life..."*

— *The Radiance Sutras: 112 Gateways to the Yoga of Wonder and Delight*, by Lorin Roche, PhD, based on the Vijnana Bhairava Tantra

Glossary of Key Tantric Terms

Shakti	Divine feminine power or energy; the dynamic aspect of consciousness; consort of Shiva.
Shiva	Pure consciousness; the still, witnessing principle; represents the masculine pole in tantra.
Prāṇa	Life force or vital energy that animates all living beings; flows through subtle channels (nāḍīs).
Kuṇḍalinī	Dormant spiritual energy at the base of the spine in the subtle body; its awakening is central to many tantric paths.
Nāḍī	Subtle energy channels in the body through which prāṇa flows; main ones are iḍā, piṅgalā, and suṣumnā.
Chakra	Energy centers or wheels in the subtle body; traditionally there are 7 major chakras aligned along the spine.
Bindu	Point of concentrated consciousness or seed; also refers to the central point in yantras or the retention of sexual energy.
Tattva	Element or principle of reality; Kashmir Shaiva Tantra discusses 36 tattvas from the gross to the subtle.

sādhana	Spiritual practice or discipline undertaken to attain realization or siddhi.
Mantra	Sacred sound or phrase used to invoke divine energies and transform consciousness.
Yantra	Geometric diagram used for worship, meditation, and invoking specific deities or energies.
Mudrā	Symbolic hand gesture or bodily position that directs energy flow during rituals or meditation.
Nyāsa	Ritual act of placing mantras or divine energies onto parts of the body.
Pūjā	Ritualistic worship of a deity, often involving offerings, mantras, and visualizations.
Tāntrika	Practitioner of tantra; may be male or female, engaged in internal or external practices.
Kriyā	In Kundalini awakening, kriyās can arise spontaneously due to increased pranic flow in the subtle body, as the body releases blockages or becomes an instrument of divine orchestration.
Siddhi	Spiritual power or accomplishment attained through sādhana. Can be worldly or spiritual.
Mokṣa	Liberation from the cycle of birth and death; ultimate goal of many tantric paths.
Samādhi	Deep meditative absorption in which individual consciousness merges with the divine. The goal of traditional aṣṭāṅgayoga.

This is Tantra

Bibliography

Anandamayi Ma. The Essential Sri Anandamayi Ma: Life and Teachings of a 20th Century Indian Saint. Syda Foundation, 2005.

Dass, Ram. Be Here Now. Lama Foundation, 1971.

Frawley, David. Tantric Yoga and the Wisdom Goddesses. Lotus Press, 1994.

Jaideva Singh, translator. Pratyabhijna Hrdayam. Motilal Banarsidass, 1977.

Jaideva Singh, translator. Spanda Karikas. Motilal Banarsidass, 1992.

Jaideva Singh, translator. Vijnana Bhairava Tantra. Motilal Banarsidass, 1991.

Kempton, Sally. Awakening Shakti: The Transformative Power of the Goddesses of Yoga. Sounds True, 2013.

Kufayev, Igor. Camatkāra: The Hidden Path. Flowing Wakefulness Press, 2020.

Neem Karoli Baba. Miracle of Love: Stories about Neem Karoli Baba. Hanuman Foundation, 1979.

This is Tantra

www.ingramcontent.com/pod-product-compliance
Lightning Source LLC
Chambersburg PA
CBHW060452080526
44584CB00015B/1417